'This stirring and prophetic work is a challenge to any reader in terms of emotion, thought spirituality, theology, humanity and practice. It respects and honours boundaries and pushes back borders that need to be pushed back and certainly crossed. This book is an important resource to all in a ministry or service of compassion.

The Revd Dr Inderjit Bhogal OBE, former chief executive of the Corrymeela Community

'*Who Cares about HIV?* is a great testament to the strength and courage of those who have shared their stories. This is a book in which the voices of individuals are heard. When I was Health Secretary in the 1980s, HIV was a virtual death sentence. We mounted a major public education campaign – 'Don't Die of Ignorance' – to explain the dangers, and we also promoted clean needles for drug users. Since then, the position has improved throughout much of the West, but HIV remains a dark cloud over the world, and a challenge for us all. The testimonies in this book help us break down the barries that people living with HIV too often face.'

Norman Fowler, the Lord Speaker

'This book makes for challenging but vital reading for the Church. There is much to be learnt from the stark tales of those who have sought care as they live with HIV. By listening to their stories we, with others across our faith communities, can be reshaped by the learning.'

The Rt Revd and Rt Hon. Dame Sarah Mullally DBE, Bishop of London

'This testimony is deeply and rightly unsettling. We must read these stories, not so that we might congratulate ourselves on the ministry that has been offered, but with contrite hearts, as a call to repentance for the role we have played in perpertuating a climate of ignorance. I wholeheartedly commend this book, and pray that we might be open to both the challenge it presents and the opportunity to encounter God in its pages.'

The Revd Canon Gareth J. Powell, Secretary of the Methodist Conference

G000022687

'*Who Cares about HIV?* is a moving testimony to the stregth, resilience and hope of the human spirit. It is also a powerful reminder that authentic ministry must address the whole person and not just the person's symptoms or diseases. The book is an equally compelling and courageous confession to the harm that can be done in the name and practice of doing good. It raises important questions for all who seek to serve others.'

Bishop Bruce R. Ough, Past President of the Council of Bishops,
The United Methodist Church, USA

WHO CARES ABOUT HIV?

Challenging attitudes and pastoral practices that do more harm than good

Stephen Penrose,
Joseph Kyusho-Ford and Paul Kybird

First published in Great Britain in 2019

Society for Promoting Christian Knowledge
36 Causton Street
London SW1P 4ST
www.spck.org.uk

British Library Cataloguing-in-Publication Data
A catalogue record for this book is available from the British Library

ISBN 978–0–281–08242–1
eBook ISBN 978–0–281–08243–8

Typeset by Manila Typesetting Company
First printed in Great Britain by Ashford Colour Press
Subsequently digitally printed in Great Britain

eBook by Manila Typesetting Company

Produced on paper from sustainable forests

But come, my friend,
Tell us your own story now, and tell it truly.
Where have your rovings forced you?
What lands of men have you seen, what sturdy towns,
What men themselves? Who were wild, savage, lawless?
Who were friendly to strangers, god-fearing men? Tell me,
why do you weep and grieve so sorely . . . ?

(Homer, Odyssey Book 8/640)

For the clients

Contents

Foreword

This is a frightening book. It has not been written with a view to making its Christian readers feel better about themselves, so it will leave a mark – a sense of unfinished business at least, a sense of being under judgement at most. The chaplaincy experience that is here described and reflected on is one that lays bare the inadequacy of trying to be 'good'. It deals with various ways in which this becomes poisonous. There is being 'good' in order to be seen as 'good'. There is the assumption that good is what I do to others who have no say about what counts as good. There is the uttering of good words that become lethal when they are not acted on. And much more. We are shown how compassion, even 'inclusion', can be instrumentalized, again and again, taking agency and dignity back into ourselves, our self-descriptions as moral and caring people or communities. The challenge posed by the experience of those living with HIV is, in other words, not just a problem with abusive, reactionary fundamentalists; it is to do with self-consciously sensitive and would-be compassionate people too, whose reactions may be as abusive in effect as many more obvious instances.

Woven throughout this book of witness is a set of intensely focused and coherent theological insights. God belongs to no one, and so is not a tool for any interest group (which is the true sense of divine 'sovereignty'). No one stands outside accountability to God or to others (which is the point of biblical language about law). God is to be met in the actuality of the other as that other expresses and embodies it (which is where the seriousness of our talk about creation and God's love of creation is tested most radically). So there is no possible engagement that is not first and foremost an exercise of what is here called 'attunement', the labour of adjusting your own preconceptions (and the agendas and anxieties they conceal) to this actuality that has to be given space and confidence to speak without editing, judgement or premature consolation. Only the narratives of those who have been hurt by the failure to work at such attunement can spell out what this really means, and that is why the personal stories here need to be read over and over.

Perhaps some of the most significant moments in the Gospel stories are where Jesus simply asks, 'What do you want?' of those who come to him. He does not begin from an interpretation of what is before him; he does not set conditions for a response in advance. By being open to attunement in this way, he displays at depth the freedom of God from all partial and protective agendas. But, paradoxically, it is natural that this then means a privilege or priority is given to those whose voices are not normally heard, those who have never been asked, 'What do you want?'

Nought for our comfort? Not a lot. I am writing these words in the wake of the first hearings of the Independent Inquiry into Child Sexual Abuse, in which I and my Church have been shown to have failed dramatically in anything that could have been called 'attunement' to those most affected by abusive behaviour and power patterns. It is impossible not to recognize the things said here as testimony to the same failings.

But avoiding the deep discomfort this brings is no answer. If our faith means anything, it must mean that confronting failure and the exposure of our 'goodness' as damaging and toxic is not the end but the start of some sort of Christian integrity. So I hope others will find, as I do, that this book is a proclaiming of the gospel as well as a call to judgement. It is necessary material for the self-examination and self-awareness of any Christian minister or community, if the Church's claim to be what it is supposed to be is not to go on being hollow for so many who need to hear that their agency and dignity are understood and honoured.

Rowan Williams

Contributors

Joseph Kyusho-Ford has been London's HIV Chaplain for ten years. He has wide experience of several world religions and his great passion in life is detective fiction. He has dedicated what he does to his grandmother, Millicent, whose goodness deserves this recognition.

Paul Kybird worked as Training and Development Officer and District Development Enabler for the London District of the Methodist Church from 2000. He has now retired from his role as Development Worker at Nuneaton Methodist Church, and served as editor for these testimonies.

Stephen Penrose set up London's HIV Chaplaincy and was its first chaplain. Now retired, he served as the Methodist minister in Abbey Wood, Peckham, Kensal Rise and Streatham. He instigated the Work and Schools Project in Peckham with young people truanting from school (the forerunner to work experience in schools), was involved with the bringing together of central London's youth work at St Martin-in-the-Fields and set up Streatham Street Link (a project concerned with the safety of women selling sex on the streets in south London).

Mark Cazalet is a contemporary artist based in London and Suffolk, UK. He trained at Chelsea School of Art and then Falmouth School of Art. Immediately after graduating, he was awarded the French government's national studentship award to study in France. He studied at L'école-des-Beaux-Arts Paris, in the studio of Christian Boltanski.

The illustrations have been funded by the MB Reckitt Trust.

Introducing the testimony

This is a 'text that burns', because here you will find the 'voice of the voiceless'. Here you will encounter the testimonies, determination, courage and faith of the clients of the London HIV Chaplaincy. Through them, a message for the institutional Church and individual Christians comes with relentless authority: that it is in the deepest darkness and the most desperate abandonment that God is truly found.

Those rendered 'voiceless' need someone to speak for them to interpret and articulate their message. In this, the chaplaincy's record is unique. It has been a journey of listening and of understanding; of humble change, as that understanding has challenged its own fundamental principles of Christian care and witness. It has resulted in a dark struggle to let the voiceless speak and to confront churches at their most sensitive point – their record of compassionate care.

The majority of the writings set out here are the work of the present chaplain. He has not been a bystander, simply watching, listening and recording. As the testimony shows, he has taken his own darker pilgrimage – one that has enabled him to hear and articulate voices that have been and would be unheard, dismissed or smothered by churches. He has also begun to develop theological reflection of a quality and ferocity that the Church urgently needs if it is to be true to its founder and the prophetic tradition from which he sprang.

In the deepening darkness of the experiences with which chaplain and clients wrestle together comes an extraordinary, radical and disturbing encounter with God. In the darkness, and through those cast into darkness not because of their sin but because they have been 'sinned against', we meet with God. So theology begins.

This is not an easy read. It is dangerous. It will and should produce a furious reaction. To read is to become involved, to change. In whatever direction you then head to take steps on a pilgrimage, it will become darker. Darker either because the message has not been heard and the challenge simply neglected, or darker because you have heard the voiceless speak and your own pilgrimage can never be the same again, as you travel with them into the shadows to discover the heart of what it means to meet God.

Why 'testimony'?

Testimony is not a form that is in common use today. It has been chosen because it is in fact the form in which the material has been received, and because of the risks that changing it would have run.

Testimony is rough edged, passionate, in your face, an encounter of the moment. It has had a long tradition in the Hebrew Scriptures, in the New Testament and in the Church since the earliest times. Testimony does not easily yield neat divisions, clean argument, guidelines for useful questions to discuss or clear rules for action plans. Its fierce, raw energy is most powerful in the spoken word of the personal encounter where the speaker's words challenge, convict and change lives. It inhabits the spontaneous moment when truth is spoken and received, in debate, in bearing witness, in worship, in the longing to grow in discipleship. It is, of course, inevitable that in written form it loses that initial pulsating power and, as a result, makes serious demands on the reader to find ways of entering into the original context and being caught up in the flow of immediate and intimate encounter.

There is another danger when testimony is turned into writing. The temptation is to render the material easier to handle, to ease infelicities of style, to remove repetitions and redundancies. But the nature of testimony is that it cannot be so shaped, directed and edited. The moment such a process begins, testimony 'dances to another tune', and another agenda, however well intentioned, begins to reshape it. The wild, the authentic, is tamed and loses its integrity.

We know the challenges of offering a difficult read, but we also know the cost borne by those whose voices speak here – voices that have already been edited into silence and absence, even by the most well-intentioned listeners, pastors or interpreters. We are desperate for you to take the journey with us and genuinely to hear their voices. We are fearful lest we diminish their cry in any way. Not to respect the reader enough to make that demand risks domestication and the production of just another booklet that sits on the shelf of the interesting and provoking, but ultimately bland.

Our conviction is that the material here is too important to take that risk. We offer testimony that puts everything 'out there', without measuring consequences and not shrinking from making mistakes or trying to speak about the hard lessons being learnt. After all, it is not a sales talk where the needs and aspirations of the audience have been carefully assessed on the journey to success. Our aim here is to make this material accessible in a way that respects its voiceless origins and reflects that power.

So this is a testimony, because those of us who have worked on this document have made a choice to stand with our chaplain in the authenticity of his choices as he bears testimony. We have chosen to listen as he shares the voices of the clients. We have chosen to listen to them with him and to attempt to let them speak. We have chosen, and the choice means a pilgrimage that is dark and grows darker. The heat is turned up, we meet a 'text that burns', whose flames are reflected in Mark Cazalet's searing illustrations.

This is our choice, so let us be clear about what this document is not.

It is not a work of literature, in which the web of words and the felicitous expression as prerequisites of a fair hearing outweigh the voices of the clients and our chaplain as their interpreter.

It is not a report, surveying the territory through quantitative or qualitative research, exploring territory with a detached academic balance and assessing a range of arguments, weighing contrasting examples and seeking a balanced, dispassionate conclusion.

It is not a work of apologetics that would contrive to add to the testifying voices a perspective of good works to create 'balance' and exonerate the Church as a whole, or individual denominations, of failure or wrongdoing.

To be clear about why we did not aim for such 'apologetic balance', and anticipating a longer conversation later in the testimony, we endorse our chaplain, who writes:

In her book, *Metaphysics as a Guide for Morals*, Iris Murdoch argues that the most fundamental aspect of the human being is not the intellectual but the ethical. It is the ability to assess information and assign it values such as true or false, good or bad.

In dealing with many parts of the Church there is an encounter with a culture of evaluation that places the institutional Church before any individual who may wish to make a complaint against it for mistreatment. That culture makes it as difficult as possible for an abused person to make their voice heard. It places a burden of proof on the abused person or (in our case) the chaplaincy rather than placing the burden of disproof on the Church. In our choice to bear testimony, the claim is more than likely to be made that our experience of the Church's pastoral care is limited and that instances of good pastoral care will serve to discredit and put into perspective the 400 cases of abuse that the chaplaincy has met. Why is it not the other way around?

Given that the Church claims a moral authority, why does not even one instance of mistreatment that has wrecked a life not call into account the claims of the Church on its own behalf to have moral authority? To me this is redolent of the attitude which says, 'Oh, I know the Church has done evil things but those are outweighed by the consolation it brings people.' This is special pleading, whatever the apologetic motivation, and is an absolute disgrace. We are helping clients who have had the life kicked out of them; we are *not* helping the Church to feel good about itself. It is as absurd as asking a report on sexual harassment to include incidences where women have not been attacked.

There is anecdotal evidence *everywhere* about 'cover-ups' by churches about sex abuse, corruption and financial misdoings. Why is it so difficult to accept clients' stories, given what we already know about church behaviour, knowledge of which is widely available in the public domain?

As chaplain, he picks up a further aspect of the choice we have made about the genre and the form of the material, tactics that have served to silence the voiceless:

During the course of the development of the work we have been beset by a Church whose mindset and apologetic tactics are used to prevent clients telling their stories through biblical images. It imposes limits on their prose descriptions and dissolves their context using psychological or linguistic filibustering. Finally, this has the effect of isolating clients from their experience by semantics alone.

A case can be made that experience is pre-verbal, and the culture I battle against attempts to run clients in circles using the net of language, the web of words. Clients are often in need of long guidance before they can articulate in the way they must if they are to get a fair hearing in such a Church culture. This is typical of institutions that wish to immure themselves from criticism or evidence of failure.

He concludes:

Values are choices. As chaplain, I *choose* to give the clients the benefit of the doubt; I choose to accept that, given the evidence on abusive religious groups that is available in the external forum, we can infer the truth of the claims of the clients. As someone seeking the good and the true, I choose to measure the Church by its claims to have a moral authority. This means I take every single instance of the possibility of wickedness, exclusion, misuse of authority and bigotry as an obligation to see if the Church acts as it speaks.

I choose to privilege the excluded, those crushed, and so I believe them first. This is not a matter of sophistry but, noting how churches treat the least and most powerless, I choose to do this and I choose to see if the Church is worth its salt. It is, after all, the Church that chooses to describe itself using the language of love . . . so where is the evidence of the shepherd leaving the 99 to seek the one, or emptying itself to become a servant?

Beginnings

In 2003, patients at the Chelsea and Westminster Hospital asked to meet with the hospital chaplain responsible for visiting the HIV directorate – not in the hospital but in the community where they socialized. By 2003, people living with HIV no longer spent long periods in hospital but lived at home in the community. Patients would come to the hospital for regular outpatient appointments.

The then chaplain, Steve Penrose, shared this with his Methodist Church colleagues, both locally and nationally, and by September 2003 the Methodist Church had made it possible for Steve to spend more time listening to people living with HIV in a more social setting. Most of the people he met with were gay men, so he would meet with them in the West End gay bars or in coffee shops. All the original clients were patients from the Chelsea and Westminster Hospital, but as time went on and news got around within the HIV community about what he was doing, more people asked to meet with him.

By 2007, Steve was meeting with more than 150 people who were living with the virus. Early in 2007 our present chaplain was seconded to the chaplaincy and worked alongside Steve. When Steve announced that he was going to retire in August 2008 (at a time when the chaplaincy was funded wholly by the Methodist Church), he and his line manager, the Revd Dr Stuart Jordan, called together representatives of all London's major church communities to explore whether or not there was a possibility of employing a full-time chaplain. The result of these discussions was that there were commitments from the Methodist Church, the Church of England, the United Reformed Church and the Roman Catholic Church to fund a full-time chaplaincy. Adverts were circulated for a full-time chaplain, interviews were arranged and a new chaplain was appointed in 2008 to succeed Steve.

The churches initially based the chaplaincy with the London Ecumenical Aids Trust (LEAT), which came under the wing of the London Churches Group, and in April 2012 it became a registered charity. In October 2012, the charity was registered as a company limited by guarantee.

The charity has its own Board of Trustees, currently comprised of 11 people, namely Baroness Richardson of Calow, Mr Bala Gnanapragasam, Mr Paul Kybird, Mr Paul Infield, Mr Kanley McHayle, Mrs Pamela Mhlophe, Mrs Odette Penwarden, Mr David Powell, Mr Nicholas Sayer (treasurer), Rabbi Mark Solomon and the Revd Steve Penrose (chair).

The Methodist Church is still a major funder of the charity, and other support is received from the Church of England and the United Reformed Church. The Tudor Trust, London Catalyst and the Big Lottery Awards for All have also funded us, and we now receive a substantial grant from The Joseph Rank Trust.

The clients' stories

The testimony of the London HIV Chaplaincy begins with human need in the face of terrible suffering and with the call that some have heard to offer a courageous and compassionate response. These stories from the beginning of the journey lead us into deep shadows. They are not easy to read. They are even harder to reflect on, and the questions they raise are difficult to live with for individual Christians and especially for churches and their leaders. Stories like these gave birth to the London HIV Chaplaincy.

The stories below are told briefly and simply. They have been chosen because they are characteristic of many of our clients. They are stories of rejection by families and by faith communities. They raise issues of governmental policies, particularly concerning the young, the poor, migrants and the homeless. With medical advances, a new need appears: the increasingly common and daunting issue of advancing age and the way it leaves people with different sorts of needs. And then there are issues of cultural blindness, superstition and gender roles, which can present themselves as the darkest and most intractable. At every point, faith communities, their people and their leaders are challenged.

To read these stories and hear them accurately, it is essential to do so in the light of this crucial warning from the chaplain, which takes us into the struggle to encounter testimony with integrity:

> As it stands, the text of these stories is too weak at presenting the requisite context in which to interpret them. There is too little material that punches directly at the abuse clients have suffered and the causes of that abuse. There is no adequate presentation of the clients' own values.
>
> In addition, we have not yet directly challenged properly the issue of the ethics of the use of information by faith communities. Taken out of context, such case studies are in danger of simply providing an opportunity for 'moral masturbation' on the part of communities who believe they are above reproach. When that happens, a process begins that can lead to validating abuse and valorizing communities that have perpetrated such abuse.
>
> My point is and will remain that the handling of clients' material risks the grave danger of being a misuse of power and

a near attempt to pervert the meaning of that material. We are too obsessed with tear-jerker or eye-catching material . . . and not with the justice of presentation.

We must be aware that our use of tragic stories does not validate faith communities as saviours of the pathetic if in fact what they point to is ineptitude and stupidity by faith communities which, in its turn, has been the cause of further suffering. It is my belief that we risk setting up the moral suffering of the client in such a way that faith communities can benefit from it. It is seen as part of a metaphor of redemption or original sin. It is not. It is abuse; abuse that is perpetrated by avoidable ignorance and well-meaning stupidity.

These stories were recorded at different times by the chaplain and/or by the Chair of Trustees.

Story 1

BC is an intelligent and articulate gay Polish man in his late twenties. He is from a Jewish background and was rejected by his family and community because of his sexuality. When he came to the UK to seek escape from his background, he was forced to take menial jobs in the so-called 'hospitality' industry, which left him poorly paid and isolated. He had no choice but to rely on his boyfriend for everything. His so-called boyfriend used him as a 'mule' for his drug dealing. The isolation, exploitation, humiliation and rejection BC experienced created an environment where he turned to drugs as a way to (in his words) 'dull the pain'.

This client has been unable to hold down a proper job, has had numerous run-ins with the police and was recently put out on the street by his boyfriend. When he came to the chaplaincy, we faced the challenges of helping him out of trouble, dealing with benefits forms and finding him counselling for addiction and other issues.

Story 2

DE is nearing his twentieth birthday and is from Liverpool. He left home at the age of 16 after severe treatment at the hands of his family because of his sexuality. He came to London to seek a better life, only to find that employment, benefit and housing prospects were at an all-time low. This client is neither wild nor a drug user; however, he turned to the 'sex trade' in order to pay bills.

Naturally, this left him open to exploitation and risky practices. He was diagnosed HIV positive seven months ago. His story deals directly with the myth that is circulating which claims that HIV is under control and infection in gay men is a result of mere 'promiscuity'. DE's case makes it clear that bad social policy can and does have health and social impacts.

On a personal level, more than anything else, DE faces terrible loneliness. Medical advances mean that he can have a long life ahead of him, but in his awful isolation he faces a desperate struggle to find any motivation to simply get on with looking to the future.

Story 3

FG is almost (but not quite) unique among the people we care for. She is North African and in her mid-seventies. She admits to living a very wild life as a younger person in Paris. That was where she contracted HIV 25 years ago. She has struggled to find meaning and purpose living with HIV and still feels very rejected and isolated. As a retired person, she has a limited income and little contact with an extended social network.

We share her story because she demonstrates that an increasing number of people live longer on HIV care and need long-term support. She has a kidney complication caused by HIV medication. She is still very private about her situation but needs urgent and ongoing personal and practical support.

Story 4

AB is West African and in her mid-forties. She moved to the UK ten years ago. She is a mother, and a nurse by profession. She is intelligent, has a great sense of humour and was heavily involved in her local Pentecostal Church.

For some time, she had problems dealing with her husband, who worked away from home, and she strongly suspected him of sexual infidelity. Her husband refused to answer any of her questions concerning his behaviour and would not countenance the use of condoms. Her attempts to seek advice from her pastor were rebuffed and it was suggested that she was 'too independent'.

Seven years ago, AB was diagnosed HIV positive. She maintains adamantly that she has had sex with nobody but her husband, and there is no reason to disbelieve her.

Her husband was in the room when she was given her test results in hospital; he stood up and walked out. Returning to the hospital later, he left her belongings in a suitcase outside her cubicle. She hasn't been allowed to see her children since that time. She has been blamed for her situation by her husband, by his family and by the pastor of her church. When she tried to seek redress, she was refused.

The rejection by her family and her church has completely undermined her confidence in herself and her ability to relate to others. Through her contact with the HIV chaplain she is beginning to regain some of her self-worth and is trying to make some sense of her life.

Story 5

'I went to see a minister for some help, having found myself HIV positive. The circumstances that meant I became infected involved a long experience of intellectual, spiritual, psychological and even sexual abuse on the part of the Church. I found myself without any faith. However, instead of exploring how I might be supported, it turned into an attempt by this particular minister to pray over me and convert me, at the end of which I still received no help.

'I found this experience quite violating and intrusive, so I discussed it with a Methodist minister friend of mine. When I told her that the other minister just tried to convert me she said, very fearlessly, "Well, what's wrong with that?" I never saw or heard from them again, and I am still struggling now.'

Story 6

'One of the things about finding yourself HIV positive is that you really don't know who you can count on for support.

'In order to get a bit of help, you open up and reach out to people. Being a gay man, I opened up to some of my gay friends, and I was shunned by an awful lot of them. I couldn't get much support from my workplace or from my faith community and found myself completely alone. The worst aspect of this was that I was so lonely and desperate that I took any friendship that was offered, which meant that I ended up being friendly with unscrupulous people who used me. They took advantage of my vulnerability and introduced me to drug use. Having tried to get me addicted by offering me stuff for free, they then tried to turn me into a drug mule.

'When I spoke about HIV to my rabbi, his response was, "You know you will find support in the gay community." But that was just not true. I approached a priest I knew and came clean about the drug abuse; he dropped me like a hot brick. If I hadn't had a good friend who helped me to kick the habit, my life would have been ruined. HIV care cannot be summed up with clichés about gender, sexuality or anything else.'

Story 7

'I have lived with HIV for many years and struggled with the isolation, the side effects of medication, the secondary medical conditions and the sheer heavy-hearted depression of being HIV positive. I decided to do something for people like me. It was my way of trying to make sense of my life, so I approached a source of support and, without being asked anything, I faced a series of exclusions that had nothing to do with my being HIV positive or with being very ill; they were based on assumptions about my gender, my skin colour and my educational level. Not once was I asked about living, nor about the sheer misery of medication and the knowledge and experience that that might give me. The criteria were based on the fact that I was male, white and university educated, and that my disabilities were hidden and not obvious. I come from a working-class background and no other member of my family has ever been to university, and yet I was treated as a symbol of privilege and I got no support. So here I am living with the effects of HIV medication, a contingent disability of a secondary disability, a history of suffering from HIV-related neurological/psychological conditions, social isolation and depression, and still no support.'

Story 8

'I converted to Christianity when I was 16, and was not really sure what I was looking for. Being an enthusiastic type, I offered myself for ministry. My training turned out to be a journey to hell. I'm the sort of person who looks at the small details, so I am a questioner, and I ask things that no one either wants to answer or can answer. It was a gateway to years of abuse of all kinds: verbal violence, rubbishing my character, psychological speculation, and even a bit of sexual abuse. The result of this long process was that I found myself HIV positive and totally messed up in my head.

'You would think that I would have walked away from religion altogether but, expecting to find answers to some of my questions, I mooched around different religions. I was totally upfront about my issues, and each time the different groups said, "Oh yes, you'll fit, we have a place for you."

'That openness lasted long enough to get me in, and then they tried to shut me up or put me on a leash. I always think of it as being collected and exhibited in someone's museum. But in the end, once I had got in, the means of repression were always the same: trashing my personality, hiding behind authority, not knowing the difference between criticism and questions, and telling lies to me. The end result is that I've been used to do the rabbi's shopping or to give a lama an interesting discussion, or I've been an object of sexual harassment at the hands of a priest, but I've never had any real support.

'There's been a way of trapping me in both my thoughts and emotions that has isolated me from my life. It has robbed me of my ability to be an agent in my own life. It has meant that I have been able to be hoodwinked, taken advantage of by a priest in my job, and left open to abusive or domineering personal relationships.

'On reflection, it seems to me that most religious professionals have appropriated the language of psychotherapy and subjectivism only in so far as it enables them to silence criticism and to stop people raising anomalies with their faith community's stories or history. In so far as religious communities have lost the concept of reality to that extent, they also isolated me from the reality of my own life.

'I have been like a rabbit in headlights, knowing what's been done to me yet not having the sense of self or the personal agency to walk away. I can now name it for what it is: abuse in the name of religion.'

Story 9

'I have lived with HIV for many years and "travelled alone" in life because of rejection by my family and my faith community. I am still seeking answers to my questions.

'I went to see a priest at a church that has a reputation for being inclusive. I believed the priest would be supportive owing to the fact that she too had been on the receiving end of bad treatment because of sexuality and gender. I honestly expected that all the talk would have been about being "accepting and open". I was very upfront about my lack of faith and about witnessing bad actions from members of the church. I made it plain that I respected the faith of others and sought to find answers for myself. The priest concerned did not react with outrage to the stories of mistreatment that I recounted, but was outraged at my lack of faith. The priest took a single half-sentence that I had said (concerning how many people *The Guardian* news-paper said attended church) and proceeded to tell me both what I thought about people of faith and that the way I was acting in my personal and private life was a result of this.

'After imputing these values to me, the priest proceeded to punish me verbally for them.

'It genuinely seemed not to enter the priest's head that I could respect alternative viewpoints; that, despite disbelief, I might seek to believe, or that I could believe in acting honourably, truthfully and kindly even if I didn't have what he defined as "faith". I got "faith" rammed down my throat when I was looking for justice, goodness, respect and truth.

'I left the meeting feeling that I had not been listened to and, more importantly, convinced that the Church had no answers to my problems. It was obvious to me that its values and mine were totally at odds . . . and that the people within the Church had no idea how to relate to different perspectives and ideologies. I will tell you now . . . I will never put a foot over the entry way to any church again.

'What I have experienced over the years has left me with grave difficulties about the nature or existence of God, and the meaning or purpose of a Church capable of covering up such bad actions on the part of its members as I had seen. In general, I have struggled to find a framework that can provide ethical or spiritual commitments for me.'

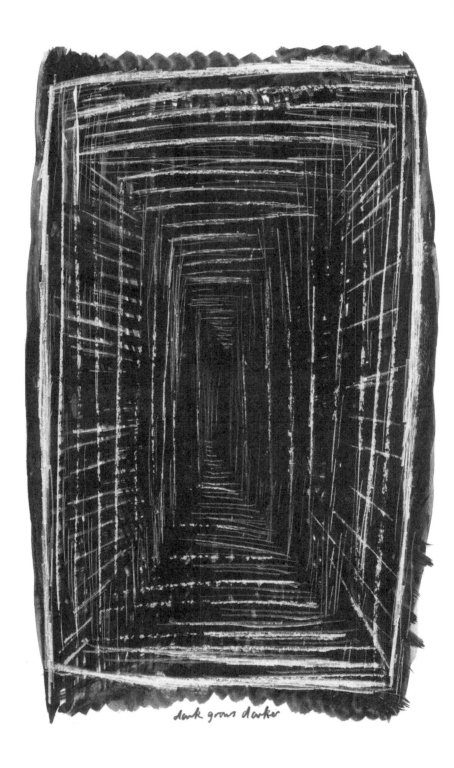

dark grows darker

First testimony
Development and learning –
the beginning of the work and some
crucial lessons

The chaplain began the work from scratch. We had no clients, and only the goodwill to try to reach out to people we thought might be in need. To put it simply, we wanted to help. We began by meeting with clients and providing pastoral care for individuals diagnosed with HIV. Clients arrived via a number of routes, and continue to do so. Some are referred by medical professionals, others from contact through faith-based agencies and some by word of mouth.

The range of clients is in itself an interesting insight into society because it includes homosexuals, bisexual men and heterosexual women, the latter often from minority ethnic backgrounds who have been infected by promiscuous husbands. At any given time, the number of clients with whom the chaplaincy is in contact is in excess of 350, though the regular contact is proportionate to the hours available.

Alongside the individual care of clients, the chaplain gives time to undertake a regular, formal reflection on the work of the chaplaincy and in particular the key issues that require attention from the wider Church. A key but difficult area of work is seeking to share insights with church leaders and breaking into the wider theological networks, for the simple reason that this area of pastoral ministry is, to say the least, on the edge. It concentrates on some of the most excluded individuals in society who face being stigmatized by their families and communities

Clients are met on an informal basis owing to the very nature of this ministry, which, as noted, is on the fringes of both society and church. All have suffered from bad experiences of the Church, and they are well informed about the many negative attitudes of the various denominations. They are, in particular, well informed with regard to the negative pronouncements of some prominent church leaders. The response of the clients to these statements means that the support offered is of a very sensitive nature.

Ideologically, we started with all the usual presuppositions about marginal clients being in need of compassion. It is also certain that we saw our main aims as twofold:

1 to provide 'emotional listening' for sick people;
2 to take a message of tolerance and compassion into faith communities and parishes.

You will notice in these aims that clients were viewed as passive objects, being 'done to' and being talked about.

The resources we took with us in the way of spiritual images were all the usual ones about the healing of lepers, the love and forgiveness of God and the need for inclusion.

Relearning listening and power

Most of us pride ourselves on being good at listening. Carers from faith backgrounds and organizations like to believe that this is one thing that makes them different from all others, but the way we talked about and practised listening in our developing situation began to reveal two problems. First, with listening, the power dynamic is rooted in the one who does the listening, and it works to detach us from the impact of the other and so raises issues of confidence and trust from the client. Second, perhaps because of that and despite our rhetoric, we actually tend to undervalue the nature and potential of the listening process. We think, and we often say, 'We have to do more than listen to people. We have to do something.'

It became obvious almost immediately that we all had to change our understanding of the term 'listening'. Clients had very good reasons not to trust faith organizations and faith communities and so we knew we would have to proceed cautiously. What was needed was more a reversal of the dynamics of listening. Instead of viewing ourselves as the ones with the answers, or with the strength to console and to impart knowledge, we had to learn to see ourselves as those with absolutely everything to learn. This wasn't only because the medical situation of people with HIV had changed but also because on every level we really did have a *lot* to learn.

If the chaplaincy were to get off the ground, the first thing we had to recognize was that we were dealing with people who felt they had never been truly listened to because the content of what they actually said was never the total focus of the response of the listener. Until we learned to privilege the speaker, and to view it as a privilege to be allowed to hear our clients' stories, we were going to get nowhere. The focus of the conversation was the speaker, and inevitably therefore the power in the relationship must lie with the speaker, not the listener.

It also quickly became obvious that clients did not want a shoulder to cry on. What they wanted was a forum in which to be heard, to be taken seriously, to have what they said acted on. The content of the exchanges was essentially prior even to the fact of the conversation. We were going to have to step up to the plate and be able to respond intelligently to the questions raised. This was really important because questions made up a huge portion of any discussions. It wasn't simply that clients were narrating their stories to a sympathetic audience. They wanted to be responded to. They wanted guidance and answers.

What they were seeking was *not* instruction. A situation where clients gave their story and were met with a long speech by the faith carer about the 'teaching of [insert here whatever label you like!]' was not going to cut any ice. What clients were seeking from us was in fact a relationship that was profoundly rooted in words. Not in emotions, but in the taking seriously of words spoken by them, and implied in this dynamic was the willingness to be changed by what we heard from them.

Far more even than that, *it meant allowing the clients themselves to interpret their own perceptions of their stories.* By this we mean that we had to take clients' concerns at face value. If clients felt that their religious faith had been a contributory factor in their being infected, we were not immediately to discount this. This was particularly important when clients brought up the fact that they were and wished to remain people who took faith seriously. The failure of the various faith communities to help them find a spiritual home was viewed as a failure of those communities rather than the failure of the clients.

Learning to be unshockable

The stories of the clients always had to start with material that could have moral labels slapped on it. This might involve sexual behaviour, addictive behaviour or emotional or psychosomatic conditions.

It was a matter of taking time to allow a whole pattern to unfold, rather than dealing with individual 'problems'. In other words, we were expected to deal with whole people and not mere sexualities, genders or sicknesses in some sort of remedial sense. The inclination to attribute a moral label to a person usually means we stop listening the moment we are faced with a certain set of behaviours. In doing so, we miss the whole flow of the person's dynamic and life. We simply fail both to make connections and to see the whole story.

We had to face situations where infidelity, acting out and despair were narrated to us. If we had arrested the conversation at any single point, we would have missed the story of the person.

Often clients could have been labelled 'promiscuous', but by doing so and then resting at that stage of the listening and caring process we would have absolved ourselves of the duty to hear and learn. We would have been able to skip the truly difficult bits that we had to learn. These often involved the failure of faith support workers to treat people in their own right, and being faced with the consequences of our own instinctive, well-meaning labelling and moralizing.

Privacy is a covenant

Very closely tied to this was allowing clients themselves to communicate as much or as little about their own lives and employment situations as they wished. We had to learn to ask little and hope they would share more as trust developed.

The chaplaincy would have been one huge spectacular failure from day one had we started asking people to fill in forms with their personal details. To do so would have created serious problems. Often partners, employers and families were not aware of clients' HIV status, and therefore we kept strictly to the principle that clients should keep their right to share as much or as little as they wished. It really is important to add that what we mean is not merely promising not to share their information, but actually *not collecting* their information. The sharing of names and postcodes with prospective funders may be necessary from a corporate or organizational point of view, but it would have caused this work to be stillborn. We decided right at the start that we would accept clients who provided as much or as little information as they wished. We kept minimal notes of addresses and, once we had agreed the terms with clients, we refused absolutely to change the deal by surrendering information to other sources. We fully accepted the clients' vulnerability. In our work with them and in the way that their views have been recorded in this document we have maintained their complete anonymity. The experiences and views reflected here have been rigorously anonymized.

Yet again, this is linked to our fundamental attitude about what we do when we undertake this kind of work. Are we providing a service to be 'used', or are we being challenged to go further in allowing people the opportunity to rebuild themselves and contribute to the faith community of which they are a part? In other words, are we the doers or the receivers when it comes to chaplaincy?

To speak and to create

Our view of chaplaincy was not one where we had 'service users', but clients who in the end helped us to create a chaplaincy. The parameters of the chaplaincy remit were dictated as a response to the needs the clients themselves felt and expressed.

Initially, we set ourselves the task of going to speak to faith communities to encourage tolerance and acceptance by education, but the clients made it plain that they wanted to be part of a wider communication with faith communities. This dialogue would involve the chaplaincy feeding back to faith communities the clients' own stories in order for those communities to learn, to be challenged and to change their responses to how they dealt with and thought about HIV.

While most clients wanted anonymity, they were still fired with a desire to make a difference. They wanted to make sure others did not suffer the same fate they had. They were determined to find meaning in their HIV status, and this meant not only existing but also creating. And what they wanted above all to create was an *equal, intelligible, learning conversation* with faith communities. Clients were not content to be mere objects of care, but wanted to be co-creators of support, learning and strategy.

Creating meaning and cultural change

The reality we began to face was that clients saw the creation of meaning as the issue, and they forced us to see the same. It began with an equal exchange of words and with them naming their own perception of their life situation in its fullest sense. It continued with the creation of a purpose and a clear goal which would affect how faith communities and institutions dealt with other people in the same situation.

The chaplaincy has often found that faith communities are willing to be flattered by the number of clients seen and then 'ticked off the list', but are far less willing to be challenged by the stories of the clients themselves if this involves the shedding of fixed pastoral reference points and real change.

Creating this new approach meant that the chaplaincy had to shift its original aim of communicating with faith communities about inclusion to a more formal and demanding stance of challenging how communities thought about HIV and dealt with people who were HIV positive. It changed our focus initially from congregations, local churches and parishes to places where future ministers and carers would be trained. But that attempt only revealed a deeper issue, for such places and courses are the fruit of deeply rooted cultures. Cultural change is the calling of prophecy. The recognition of our change of stance inevitably meant a change of purpose. We had to change from 'sticking plasters' to prophecy, and to do that we had to let the voices of the clients be heard. It is that which motivated us to share their stories and their words and to make the attempt both to articulate their message and to reflect on it theologically in a way that enables the voices of the hitherto voiceless to challenge the cultures that dominate contemporary church life.

stories of rejection

Second testimony
Pastoring shock – the chaplain describes meeting with clients and hearing their stories

My purpose is to tell the stories and share the insights gained from ten years of working in the HIV field. The stories are from people who were willing to be open and share their lives with me and through me with the wider community. I make no attempt to offer any apology for an end result that may be a bit blunt and raw edged, especially for members of churches. We venture to a place of darkness. We must resist the temptation to run from it. Only by waiting and listening can we understand and feel the shock and pain of constant darkness.

Accepting the darkness

Each client told a similar story as their darkness deepened. It was the desire to talk. It wasn't the desire to be agreed with – it was simply the need to explore issues and, above all, to do so in communication with another individual.

My clients have all been remarkably self-aware about their motives in seeking to communicate. They have looked to explore very definite issues and have sought a two-way process. They had very definite questions. They did not wish to be told what to do; instead, they desired understanding and a safe place in which their questions might meet a reflective response from someone prepared to be a companion with them on their journey. At this point the greatest challenge arrived. The clients were not seeking 'empathetic' listening designed to make them feel better at some level. Instead, with extraordinary courage, they were intent on the exploration of specific answers to their specific questions. They have been plunged into darkness and would not accept answers that avoided the challenge of that darkness.

Accepting gender, sexuality and relationship

To engage honestly with their questions, one quality above all others is essential for listener and client alike: acceptance when it comes to the areas of sexuality and gender. All clients put to me the need to talk about their experiences. In the case of each of my clients, their first port of call with their questions had been the leader or pastoral carer of their particular faith community, usually a member of the clergy. All bore testimony to a response of embarrassment and resistance. This was clearly evident in two examples of ways in which ministers and pastors responded to working with clients: 'I don't need to listen to people; I just need to love them,' and, 'If you have to talk about faith, it suggests that somehow you don't believe.'

Both attitudes provide no dialogical basis for relationship and indicate the jarring embarrassment of leaders who think religion is only 'within' and that – service expected to their church apart – faith makes you entirely self-contained. It was the resistance of leaders who actually fail to recognize that we meet God in the space *between* two people. God is not 'owned' by one person in any encounter or any confrontation. God is met there. This is the one issue that has cast its shadow over every pastoral encounter and has caused more embarrassed looks and shifting of chairs over the years when I have tried to talk to faith communities about my work.

The search for specific, unrestricted dialogue

The clients fall mainly into two categories: first, gay men and second, women who feel additionally the pain of restriction as women in their faith communities. There are also some who would identify themselves as bisexual, however, and others who are heterosexual.

As they recalled the experience of presenting their questions to faith leaders, what was distinctly surprising about these questions was that they did not seem in any case to have their origins in guilt or self-hatred.

One client summed up his initial attempts at communication about faith issues like this: 'I wanted my minister to tell me why, if God had allowed me to be gay, or even made me this way, the Church was so opposed to it.'

Such a question is profoundly self-accepting and seeking a dialogue that would involve a search for answers. The client was in search of an experience of equality where his specific situation would be the focus of the discussion, and the response he was looking for was a genuine attempt to answer his questions.

This kind of story has been repeated to me time and again by clients. It did not matter precisely what the subject concerned – it could be the use of contraceptives in a situation where a woman's husband was suspected of infidelity, the genesis of sexuality, or the reasons why clients felt restricted in their marital and/or church lives because of their gender. In all cases, the clients reported feeling remarkably free (indeed, at times, I privately thought, naïvely so) to present their stories and to find understanding. It is true that they expected answers to their specific questions, but they neither seemed to wish to be congratulated nor approved of every aspect of their person. They did, however, expect a specific dialogue true to their specific issues and questions. They came to the pastoral moment in confusion, but that was not the same thing as self-hatred. They came keen to ask questions, but not with an attitude of aggressive criticism. They came with disappointment and frustration at their struggle to find acceptance, but that was most certainly not the same thing as anger.

In every single one of more than 300 cases, clients reported that the reception they received in seeking wisdom was the restriction of the terms of their dialogue by the listener.

If the question raised was sexuality, then most often the response on the part of pastors was dogmatic prohibition. Whatever aspect of spiritual teaching they might have resorted to at that point, to put it bluntly, they refused to talk about sex. If it was gender role, then very often the person was treated with an uncomprehending harshness born of panic, as if they were 'a mouthpiece for the devil', or of 'Godless' Western secularism.

All clients reported that the specifics of their questions were deflected on to broader, generalized questions that were dogmatic, cultural or nonspecific to them. As one client put it, 'It was as if the minister was fighting the Church's cultural wars in me.'

Clients felt that, instead of being treated as individuals, they were treated as issues, and these issues were seen explicitly as rebellions against faith and teaching. One female client put it like this: 'I was told that even to ask about resisting my husband showed that I watched too much "satanic" television, and that I was falling into the grasp of the devil.'

This is an example of an extreme response in the way the dialogue was shut down (or not even started), but this client is not alone in admitting that even to ask questions was met with accusation. When ministers or pastors do this, they stigmatize natural reactions and they cause people, or even force them, to be angry.

Suffocation and blame: the pastoral tragedy

When I explored with clients their feelings about God or the Church, it was amazing to discover that they all were and are people seeking to maintain a balanced faith and to live with integrity in their own situation. Our clients are not out to attack the Church, but to question and seek answers within the faith community. The treatment they received from those of whom they sought pastoral care effectively shifted responsibility from the institutions on to the individual.

There are two preliminary points I noted that apply to all faiths and cultures. First, the gender, sexuality or race of the pastor has *never made a significant difference* with regard to the quality of care the clients have received. Second, while the main focus of experience is on the Church, we are actually dealing with a 'multifaith' issue. There are clients who have left their faith communities and tried other religions in a search for a more authentic way to deal with the questions they have. The quality of care did not improve. They were then left with the additional issue of coping with the near-universal failure of religious groups in London to account openly for the inadequacy of (or in some cases inaccuracy in) religious narratives that led to the failure of care. Their experience also highlighted how religious communities can be very slippery when it comes to the meaning of words and the use of language in their accounts of their respective narratives.

With one client, I explored her feelings and thoughts about the whole process. She said, 'I hate the Church now, but I have never hated God. I approached my minister precisely because I felt accepted by God. It is the Church, not God, that has rejected and alienated me.'

One client put his experience like this:

Every time I went near someone for advice it was like having a pillow put over my face. I was being suffocated to death. In the end I just stopped trying. I lost all hope that anything I had to say would ever be taken seriously. Since that time I have experienced low self-esteem, self-hatred and anguish. I blamed myself for being different, for asking the wrong questions, for never fitting in.

It was fundamental to the way I later evaluated clients' stories to realize that that self-hatred wasn't an inherent or intrinsic part of the clients' identity. They had all *learned* to hate themselves as a result of a total failure of communicative relationships on the part of church pastors. If people are told often enough that they are evil, outcast, unfit or stupid, then they become so in their own mind. That is certainly the case with the clients who shared their experiences of their churches' pastoral care, and it is unarguably a terrible dereliction of pastoral responsibility

Pastoral refusal by generalization or stereotyping

The presenting issues with all clients were connected with either sexuality or gender, and all clients reported refusal by a pastor to meet within a context of equality that would allow them to deal with the specifics of their own case. Instead, the conversation moved quickly into a pattern of generalization, and this resulted in the *imputation* of issues that were not being raised by them and which had no direct connection with their HIV diagnosis later in their lives.

It is important to note that in all cases the clients were discussing issues *before* HIV diagnosis. It is not surprising that the clients saw the responses they then received to their HIV status as part of an entire process of a lack of communication where they were never allowed to raise specific questions in their own right and where their questions were either brushed aside or treated with contempt.

Even when they sought a specifically spiritual remedy, the response was given almost always in a way that generalized the person rather than treating them as an individual. Again, in the words of a client:

> When seeking advice about alcohol abuse I was repeatedly told that God loved me no matter who or what I was. When I suggested that in that case God didn't seem to love or be interested in *me*, I was told that I didn't have enough faith.

Pastoral refusal by isolation and denial of wholeness

A further key issue that constantly presented itself when listening to clients' reports of their pastoral encounters stood at the other pole from the tactic of generalization. Most of them felt and thought that, through the pastoral encounter, individual parts of their personal life stories were isolated from the whole. This isolation had inevitably come to shape their understanding of themselves. In particular, this was true in the realm of sexuality.

One client reported that sex acts were treated as isolated 'moral' incidents with no reference to cause or to the whole context of his life:

> I had become sick and tired of getting no answers and help, so I had sex with someone in a fit of despair. The only thing people suggested was going to confession. The priest spoke of the evils of sex and said God forgave everything, I shouldn't worry. By the way, nobody listened to my expression of despair and nobody suggested an HIV test.

While the discussion of sexuality was the most obvious area where this pattern occurred, it also appeared in the areas of substance abuse, volatile emotional life (expressed as extremes of anger, despair or depression) and eating disorders. Clients reported multiple responses from faith carers that included faith healing, exorcism and confession/repentance.

In this context, eating disorders presented surprisingly frequently. When clients mentioned these, they were treated as issues that should be remedied by asceticism in the case of overeating or, in the case of bulimia, by attempts to bolster self-esteem by reminding the client that 'God loves you'.

One client put their story like this:

> When I explored the issue of my bulimia with the pastor he told me that God loved me no matter who or what I was; he didn't bother to explore what I was or find out why I thought I was such s***. He certainly didn't connect the issue to the lack of free discussion of sexuality and, more importantly, to the lack of freedom to talk about these issues.

Again and again, clients told stories that showed issues around physicality, emotionality and rebellious behaviours were treated in isolation and not connected to the whole person. They were driven to a point where they felt they had to stand their own ground and assert themselves with whatever energy was available to them. Such responses resulted in actions such as drug-taking or self-harm, which were then used to criminalize or pathologize them. The profoundly challenging irony of this situation is that it is the very spirit of rebellion that keeps clients alive!

The story of a very specific client sums up all the stories. The client had sunk into despair and recounts alcohol and substance abuse that resulted in what was initially thought of as colitis. The client approached a priest, who laid hands on the client for the healing of the physical condition. When the condition persisted, the client reported:

> I went back and said I still had my tummy trouble and, in fact, it was worse. The priest told me I lacked faith. When I tried to link my physical condition to my despair and anguish over not being talked to, the priest walked out of the confessional.

The issue is this: in all cases, the clients were being treated as isolated symptoms rather than whole persons. Emotions and behaviours were stigmatized rather than connected to the whole personality of the individual. Ultimately, there wasn't the will or the ability to seek causal connections in order to understand and in turn increase the clients' understanding of themselves and help them to a place of wisdom in dealing with their specific situation.

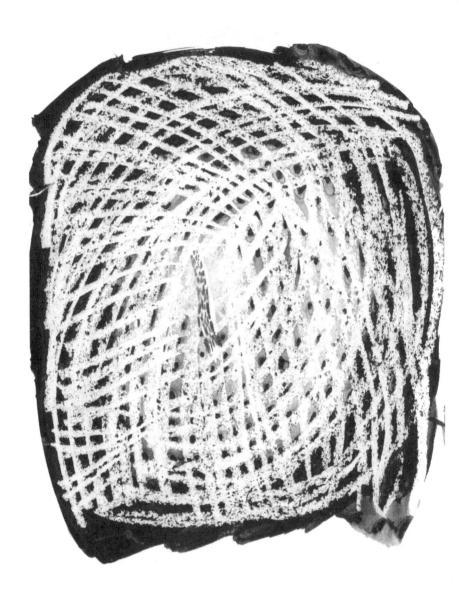

completly alone

Third testimony
And so to HIV

This section of the clients' stories centres on the care they received when they tried to broach the subject of their status in order to seek the resources to live with and make sense of being HIV positive. The chaplain describes their experiences.

The imputation of immorality

The first and most important issue that arose was what one client called 'imputation'. It is closely related to the tactic of generalization, stereotyping or 'universalization' – the process via which churches try to make everyone the same. She describes her experience in the following way:

> Going to discuss with the minister my recent diagnosis – he never bothered to ask me how I think I got infected but instead started talking about the effects of an immoral lifestyle. In fact, I was infected by an unfaithful husband, but that didn't seem to enter his head. It was assumed from the outset that I had been a 'loose woman' and that in some fundamental way I deserved what my actions had brought on me.

This is not a unique story. All of the clients reported that the first reaction they received when they sought advice was a lecture about morality. If the client was gay, sexual activity with many partners was automatically assumed. One client remarked, 'I had had sex with one guy but the priest kept talking to me as if I had slept with a thousand.'

A number of women clients are bringing up children who are HIV positive. In an attempt to seek pastoral advice, one client revealed her own HIV-positive status and the pastoral worker immediately lectured her on the fact that HIV was 'God's punishment for sexual immorality'. As a result, she backed off and didn't bring up her child's status.

The words that appeared as 'keywords' from pastors or from people of faith supposedly offering support in this kind of case always seemed to be words such as 'promiscuity' or 'punishment'.

Being gay was always treated negatively. One client said, 'The pastor compared being gay to being a drug addict.'

When I have given talks to clergy, I have been dumbfounded to hear comparisons between homosexuality and alcoholism, and between homosexuality and mental illness.

Such responses destroyed the clients' ability to trust or open up and, frankly, that is no surprise. The clients' stories were not being heard. Instead of receiving careful listening to their attempts to recount their own versions of events, they found themselves ignored, either actively or unconsciously, and on the receiving end of diatribes about immorality.

'Lepers, sinners, whores' and all that

The next topic that clients wanted to dwell on (and with considerable anger, I might add) was the spiritual and pastoral tools used by even sympathetic pastors or carers. Effectively, all these images were 'disempowering' ones. While they were part of the spiritual traditions of the various faith communities, they were so often applied indiscriminately and irresponsibly that it boggles the mind.

One female client recalls, 'The first image used to supposedly help me was that Jesus accepted whores and sinners. Well, frankly, I am no f****** whore.'

This reaction was met with similar anger and frustration when the image of lepers was used. Clients (particularly women) were profoundly unhappy to be categorized as outcasts and terminally ill people, because none of them was in a situation of facing death when they approached someone for help. They were (in the words of a male client):

> . . . trying to find ways to reincorporate myself into life, to get on with my life. I was not looking to take up residence in a leper colony, nor indeed to view myself as a healed leper. I wanted to be a person, pure and simple.

HIV is now categorized as a chronic condition, not a terminal one. That so many pastoral carers go instinctively to such images simply displays a lack of knowledge about the situation of those living with HIV.

Clients need images that offer a dynamic towards reclaiming their lives, and opportunities to relate to others as equals. What they do not need are images that keep them locked in an eternal 'pity party', where the traditions and narratives of faith force them towards celebrating a victim status.

The 'healing' path

Among the most disturbing phenomena faced by clients were responses that were offered in the form of spiritual healing or, in extreme cases, exorcism. It is not our purpose to tackle the complex questions and theologies surrounding the ministries and claims of healing in various parts of the Church. What I want to highlight is the pressure some clients felt to agree to undergo some form of healing ministry and then, in some cases, even to sign certificates attesting to their healed status, the end result of which is still to have a perpetual label of being 'healed'. One female client expressed her story like this:

> I felt that my church was not interested in me as a person but, rather, as a way to win prospective converts or members by parading my [healed] status around. In other words, I felt like an object, a trophy that was used to prove the power or truthfulness of my church's teaching.

Not all faith communities resorted to healing practices with the same enthusiasm or in the same way. Several clients reported that healing services were completely anonymous. By that I do not mean that clients didn't have to display their identity to the wider community (which most didn't want to do anyway); rather, the healing services were separate from any additional provision for the clients to express their stories by simply talking. One client called it 'the conveyor-belt system of healing. I felt that by trying to talk, to have my voice heard, I was in some way being an "inconvenience".'

A key feature was, I noticed, common to all these cases. It was the focus only on the diagnosis of HIV. Nothing was done to care for the whole person and to restore a dynamic of communication. Nothing was done by faith communities to incorporate the specifics of clients' stories in ways that cared for the *whole person*. Clients felt judged, ignored, stereotyped or used.

In search of guidance: ever-increasing circles

Clients were not content to restrict their quest for guidance and inspiration merely with regard to dialogue (or the lack of it) with clergy, pastors or faith carers. In fact, most clients reported that, in the absence of suitable guidance, they would very often read about HIV and its associated issues in the hope of getting some help. They were very far from being passive victims. I am impressed with the amount of sheer determination and energy they as a group put into searching out sources of help.

During their adventures in reading, however, clients reported many of the same experiences. In the words of one client:

> Every time I read a comment, a sermon or piece of reflection on HIV I felt used. It was as if I was a pawn in some great chess game that churches were playing. Most often the existence of HIV was used to demonstrate that certain kinds of sexual activity were 'punished by God'. Alternatively, the very fact of HIV was used to assert that the 'world' had drifted into Godless secularism and that the faith communities were right after all in asserting that the world needed them.

At its worst, some material seemed to take the line that HIV was the 'natural' end-product of seeking to empower women or gay people.

It wasn't just that clients were discouraged by the tone or content of the more hard-line reflections on HIV. Equally, some clients did not respond well to material that purported to be sympathetic. This included sermons or articles that used patronizing images or had the ultimate effect of lowering self-esteem. One client said, 'I heard a well-known woman bishop speak about "inclusion". She seemed to work out of a sliding scale of wretchedness. The groups that she wanted churches to include were "prostitutes, women, gay men and women, people with HIV".'

Instinctively, the client did not want her story or status conflated with every object of misery. That path can only end in depression and no self-esteem.

The experience of many clients is expressed by a gay man who went to hear a sermon in hope of encouragement: 'The preacher said that although God didn't create rubbish he did collect it. HIV was one of the categories the preacher included among the "collectibles".'

It is clear from the clients that the end result of all such 'well-meaning' compassionate approaches was that their self-image remained extremely poor and they constantly associated their status with being one of a class of 'poor unfortunates'. Their status was used to demonstrate why the moral teaching of faith communities was correct, particularly in opposition to the secular world. In turn, they felt used by communities who thought that inclusion demonstrated the accepting generosity of their community. This was clear when the experience proved to be one of mere tolerance by the community rather than mutual listening that led to careful reflection. One client put it this way: 'It was like they thought they were doing me a favour by accepting me, that it showed me how good they were.'

One female client brought home the reality of the situation in vivid terms: 'I heard that one bishop said that he had actually touched people with HIV, and then proceeded to score points against his theological enemies who had not even met anyone with HIV.'

The consequences in the whole Church

All of the above suggests that in some ways faith communities can all too easily adopt a proprietorial but false attitude when they have publicly addressed the issue of HIV. I am reminded of comments preceding a visit to the UK of a well-known Church leader in 2010: 'The Church understands HIV. It provides most of the front-line care of patients in Africa. The Church understands HIV!!'

Are my clients and I mistaken in hearing 'the Church owns HIV' as the subtext in the way this is presented?

I have encountered this myself when trying to talk to well-known faith carers. More than once when I have tried to address the issue of HIV care I have been faced with an approach that uses patronizing imagery, that gives pastoral care by generalizing, isolating and stereo-typing, or that simply ignores the specifics of cases. When faced with the sort of challenges the clients bring, more often than not the end result is simply silence.

One client expressed it this way: 'It struck me that all my rabbi really wanted was for me to "get involved" in the community. Acceptance seemed to mean silence.'

Again, a Buddhist client said, 'It seemed to be decided for me what care I needed. It was like I was being told, "We know you better than you know yourself."'

In everything above, we see that the responses of representatives of faith communities are working out of a different set of metaphors and symbols from the ones used by our clients. Pastors are presuming that all that people need is to feel better and to be included. Clients want answers to their questions about specific narratives, anomalies and lack of knowledge on the part of faith communities.

This is summed up in the most absurd example I ever heard from a pastor: 'People are just looking to belong. It is why they follow football or sports teams.'

Actually, *no* clients were aiming for that. They are trying to make sense of their world and are willing not to belong if necessary.

desire to talk

Fourth testimony
The chaplain describes images used by the clients to craft and express their own story

There is nothing that leaves us more vulnerable, more open to being misinterpreted or misunderstood, than putting on paper those precious, private images and symbols each of us uses to find and express meaning.

Even so, in this testimony we didn't feel that we had any choice *but* to include a section describing the images and symbols through which clients were forced to narrate their stories, for two reasons: first, because the task of the chaplaincy has been to help people articulate their 'religious situation'; and, second, because if this testimony is to have any real impact, it must challenge faith communities and individuals to truly to hear the clients' own 'telling of meaning' in order to develop stories that those communities can use to understand themselves anew as those living with HIV are embraced.

The power of these stories is not only their own deep integrity, forged as they are in some of the darkest places of human experience, but also that they are born of the Church's story and traditions. The Bible, of course, is a regular resource and its stories and characters emerge renewed. If the Church can listen carefully enough, the ways in which the images take new directions can enable it to hear the voice of prophecy once again, recalling it to its gospel roots and refining treasured traditions so that it can speak in new and urgent ways.

As we have seen throughout these words of testimony so far, there is another perspective that makes the task of hearing terribly significant. The images that have once given life and meaning, and in some circumstances still do, can nevertheless become tyrannical and unbending tools to subdue and humiliate those on the margins. The material the chaplain records and reflects on in the sections below once again offers the choice of life or death, light or darkness.

In the 'image of God'

The first sets of images I want to look at are best held together by the idea of implicit dignity, or 'creation in the image of God', as found in the Creation narratives of Genesis 1—2.

Despite the complex and controversial ways in which the stories have been used in faith communities, not least in the gender domination associated with Adam, it is the case that among our clients, creation in the image of God was the first and favourite image with which to begin religious reflection.

Both men and women used the story to establish their own dignity by speaking of being 'made in God's image'. They didn't dwell on gender implications or differences in their use of these stories. They simply referred to Adam as an archetype for their own sense of dignity that was given to them by no other human being, institution or body.

At this point lay a surprise. In every discussion, the clients seemed to take for granted that, when they discussed this with us, God was present. There were absolutely no clients who were uncomfortable with God 'walking' with humans in the garden (see Genesis 3.8). The question of God's existence was simply not raised. The existence and goodness of God who would walk with them, and creation by God as an expression of inherent dignity, was a given.

Even so, this image from and of the Garden of Eden was not one that was unproblematic in the clients' minds. It is important to say first of all that clients didn't use this image in a naïve way. Eden was not a synonym for having no emotions, not needing love, 'being angelic'. Quite the contrary, in fact: clients seemed to resort to this image *precisely* to affirm their own humanity, and most spent a great deal of time 'unpacking' the contents of this archetype of humanness with the help of other biblical images.

Interpreting humanity: questions to God

It was not unexpected to find at the top of the list the biblical image of Job. In the reflections of the clients he was an example of suffering that 'bit back'. In particular, Job was used as a vehicle to answer God back, to challenge God over an experience of silence or God's failure to act against the 'Job's comforters' that surrounded them in their lives. Clients seemed particularly able to use Job to challenge anyone who suggested that questioning was unacceptable as an aspect of the life of faith.

Tied to this characteristic and deployed in the same way were the images of Moses and Abraham, both of which were used consistently as examples of arguing with God about how sinfulness or differences were approached and judged.

The clients resorted to these biblical characters in a quite straightforward manner, presuming without question that if Moses (Exodus 32.11) or Abraham (Genesis 18.23) could argue with God, so could they. We never came across a single client who felt that these images were hierarchically superior to them. In the minds of the clients, these were exemplars not of special people, but of people full stop. The interesting thing to note was that all the images the clients identified with were 'relational' and those that moved them to internal or external 'relationship'.

Joseph: the abused dreamer

A fascinating biblical character used by clients to comment on their own situations was the character of Joseph from the book of Genesis (Genesis 37.39—50). I was very surprised that they were not put off by a character who might seem rather precocious. He was a favourite, especially among our female clients, as someone who had dreams from God which were *given* to him, not asked for or sought. He was seen as being treated appallingly by those whom he should have been able to trust: his father and brothers who, in different ways, were all abusive to him.

Joseph became a figure to enable the naming of experiences of rejection by those in authority, when all the clients had sought was to understand what God wanted of them. The clients used Joseph to express two things: first, that they were expressing a dignity they felt was 'natural'; and second, that they had experienced being treated with an abnormal severity that they felt was not deserved. Joseph enabled them both to affirm their own dignity and to judge others' response as failure.

Female images

Female clients developed their own set of images very explicitly in reaction to the 'sinners and prostitutes' images that they encountered in the pastoral care offered to them. They were possibly the most creative group when it came to developing their own images. They didn't subvert images they had received from the Church. They quite simply rejected the images offered outright! The characters they chose most frequently were Judith (book of Judith) and Tamar (Genesis 38; Matthew 1.3). Other characters they related to were Rahab (Joshua 2.6; Matthew 1.5), Jael (Judges 4; 5.24), Hannah (1 Samuel 1—2), Vashti and Esther (book of Esther) and, surprisingly, Miriam the sister of Moses (Exodus 15.20–21).

As we reflected with the clients about their use of the images, what became obvious was that each of the characters was powerful and active, but misjudged. Seemingly weak or immoral, in actual fact all were leaders and asserted their own character within very restricted situations. Suggesting reading material around these figures and discussing impressions afterwards provoked some of the most stimulating conversations we had with clients.

Liberation and dignity

A point certainly not examined by the clients in their reflections with us was how we perceive our dignity. Is it simply 'there' or do we become aware of it when situations arise to rob us of it? I raise this because the next image clients related to was one of 'liberation'.

The favourite set of images resorted to was from the book of Exodus. Clients used this in two ways. The first was certainly to assume that God 'saw' their suffering and would act to help them. The second was the use of the texts surrounding this theme to give themselves permission to express their suffering to God.

It was this second use that caused most resistance when the clients resorted to these images with pastors and church leaders. It was also something we encountered when talking about our work in groups. There appears to be a knee-jerk reaction among many church leaders and members to 'defend God's honour' by asserting that recognition or expression of pain is a redundant part of any dynamic in any relationship, especially in a spiritual one.

The Exodus story was used by clients to give them permission to recognize their emotional, physical and situational suffering, *and* to legitimize the expression of those identified conditions. Their purpose in expressing them was to seek to be liberated from them by seeking redress and action from themselves, others and God. The clients' uses of these images were not merely internal. They were expressly about changing their actual lived situations.

One final reflection is appropriate here. Clients identified with some prophetic images to explain their internal anguish and to source it in God. When challenged as to why they simply didn't walk away from faith altogether, they explained that the images of anguish and faithfulness were found in major biblical prophets, such as Hosea and Jeremiah.

Yet again we see that, far from using texts to justify the absence of a relationship, clients were using them to situate broader aspects of their own experienced humanity within the context of relational situations. They were using these images to explore the implications and expressions of aspects of their dignity.

Another set emerged that was more explicitly 'communal' and focused around God's law.

The law of God, King, Protector, Adviser

This was a surprise. All the clients had been given the image of the 'law of God' as a means of closure when they raised questions about their own situations. Yet clients found and creatively used the images surrounding 'law' frequently and very effectively.

In the first place, law was in the clients' minds not merely as something that they themselves were subject to. It was something that communities and teachers were themselves under. God was in that sense not seen or related to merely within themselves as the clients' own private source of affirmation, but was, rather, a transpersonal and social image that established multiple connection relations. The image of God's law given for God's people expressed that perfectly.

It was in this sense that the image of God as 'King', 'Protector' or 'Adviser' arose in discussions. Central to these ideas as the clients used them was that God was the possession of no one, least of all communities and leaders. In fact, God was not related to as a mere function of the self, but was an animating social principle.

The other interesting thing that arises from reflecting on this was that it was primarily used as a tool for criticism of the internal life of the faith communities to which the clients belonged. These images were used in a very reflective way to enable the expression of discontent and the raising of questions about the structure and conduct of community life. The points they made were directed towards hierarchy and were explicitly 'contemporary'.

As with the previous image of the Garden of Eden, clients need other images to tease out what they thought this 'law' might actually mean. At the top of the list of images used were the biblical prophets. The call to protect the marginal and those on the fringes of communities were about the only times clients identified to an image of themselves as marginal. Based on this call, as far as the clients were concerned the faith communities were not free to ignore the command of their religious heritage that the excluded were to be included. This led inevitably to a fierce dose of fault-finding with pastors and authority figures. This is hardly surprising, as the biblical prophets are littered with attacks of the most cutting variety with regard to the behaviour of community leaders. Our clients seemed very adept at accessing these as a means to give vent to an experience of one-sidedness in the relationship between themselves and community leaders.

While these texts were often used with great fury and determination, it was impressive that the dynamics of reflection were never simply to 'annihilate' opponents or to discredit faith communities. Instead they served as images of the self-criticism that communities need to survive, and their purpose was expressly remedial in nature. Far from the clients merely engaging in a selfish, vengeful 'rant', the purpose was always ethical in the best sense of the word.

Apocalyptic images: a mechanism of hope

Finally, we come to the most uncomfortable of the texts used by clients. These are the ones that at first tried the chaplaincy's tolerance and tested its open-mindedness! These are the 'apocalyptic' texts.

A favourite way for clients to express their discontentment and disillusionment with the general situation of themselves and indeed of the world was to relate to the prophet Daniel or the book of Revelation. I distinctly remember the sheer embarrassment and distaste I felt the first time a client used these. I wanted nothing more than to 'explain them by explaining them away'!

Given the nature, context and temptations involved in turning to images from apocalyptic literature, it is vital to note that clients did not resort to these texts in any ways that were paranoid or delusional. In all the chaplaincy's experiences, only a single client has connected these images to personal 'visions' or antisocial paranoia.

When clients were asked to talk about why they identified with these texts, it became obvious that two things were happening. First, they were using them as permission to express the sheer unmitigated disillusionment they felt with faith communities, but without being in the situation of having to choose to be people without faith. Their trauma is reflected in the ways in which the persecuted communities that found radical hope in the heroic stories of the first part of Daniel found similar resources in the story of the defeat of the hidden malign powers at work in this world, the inevitable cost of that battle to God's suffering people and the intervention on their behalf of the figure of the 'Ancient of Days' and the 'Son of Man' in the second part of the book.

Second, the clients were not being irrational but, rather, were following apocalyptic tradition in expressing an almost unlimited hope in the possibility of change in the future. Whether the subject matter was engagement with the persecuted or outcast, or the remedy of social and political injustice in a renewed community, these texts were used to provide a mechanism of hope and healing as glimpsed in the final chapter of the Revelation to John, though not, of course, in isolation from the tormented experience of the earlier chapters.

Against the 'labels': a conclusion of a sort

Further elements of this material need to be highlighted.

First, what was never discussed was the belief that God was absent, didn't exist or was otherwise not available. The clients, while angry and critical, were never dismissive of the importance of the faith. They were not living up to the label of being 'faithless'.

Second, every single image used was relational in its primary context. Whether the client was trying to integrate aspects of their own emotional, physical or communal experience, there was always a relational aspect which was very far from the 'selfish and self-absorbed' label these clients often receive. We found that the issue of an actual, communal, 'in-this-world' relationship was at the forefront of their reflections. They were not interested in merely 'feeling better'.

God functioned as a symbol not of individualized feelings of safety or comfort but, rather, of challenge and communal responsibility. We are in no way removing the desire for personal integration or wholeness from that picture. However, in their reflections, it was the clients themselves who put the need and impulse in a communal setting.

Finally, and perhaps most importantly, almost never did the clients resort to images of marginalization to reflect on their situations, except that they felt marginal to the life of communities. They never used images that repressed themselves, nor did they wallow in self-pity. One of the most important theological points of this entire reflection is how the image of God in clients' lives served as the irrepressible force of action and restoration of relationships.

On a personal level, as I wrestle with this material alongside the stories of the clients, it becomes obvious that we are being faced with the deliberate failure or inability to relate to a whole section of people in a healthy way. The result of this is, I would argue, the generation of depression, self-destruction and hypocrisy as a direct result of the failure of a two-way relationship. We are witnessing the *frustration of a desire for relationship*, which has devastating consequences for individuals and faith communities.

There is a warning in all of this material. Not once did people with HIV use images about their weakness or their sexuality, but only about their person. We must not colonize their minds.

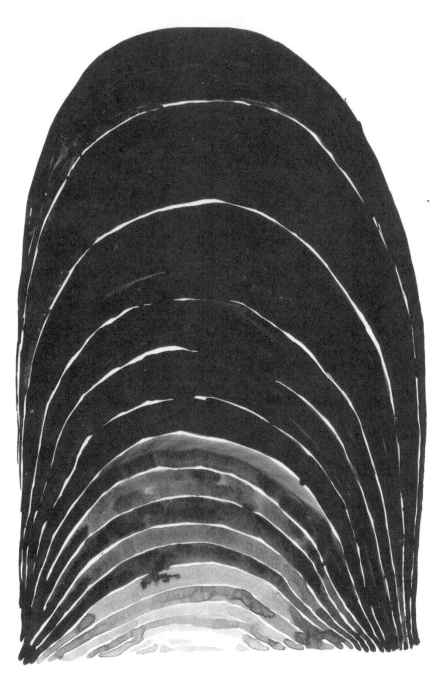

suffocated to death

Fifth testimony
Talking to clergy and leaders

During the first three years of work, our chaplain met 180 clients. They were from backgrounds in which religious faith was very significant. The majority were Christian, but there were Islamic, Jewish and Buddhist clients as well. The roles faith and its institutions, particularly churches, played in their lives were therefore of profound significance. In this section of his testimony, the chaplain sets out to give an account of how churches in particular have responded and continue to respond to the pastoral and theological challenges posed to them by HIV. It is a dark story and grows all the darker under the passionate and rigorous analysis he offers. At the root of this analysis is the tragedy of the way the solution becomes the problem.

In 2011, our chaplain put together a series of talks in which he set out to share the voices of the clients with clergy groups. A composite version of them is reproduced here.

Part 1: Reflecting on method

The method I have employed has been strictly dictated by circumstances. The first of these is the fact that many clients came to see me *after* having consulted therapists of varying approaches, and having found the results unsatisfactory. They carry with them the scars of those encounters.

Second, I work with the conviction that, despite all the other factors involved in a person's development, what we believe or think forms how we see the world and how we see ourselves. This in turn influences how we act. To me, at least, that is totally self-evident, but nearly *all* of the 180 clients in my care at that time found that their *faith* had been automatically discounted or brushed over. Instead, influences were imputed or theorized that bore no correspondence to the way they themselves described their own stories or how they experienced their own inner development. It wasn't only therapists who had done this. Those responsible for attempted spiritual care were often the worst offenders.

At the root of the problem is spiritual care based on a notion of 'love' that is misdirected. It prevents clients from facing fundamental questions directly. As a result, the search for the truth is shaped by a 'mother love' syndrome that is too often employed by churches when dealing with questions they do not wish to (or are not able to) answer.

So when I say that the London HIV Chaplaincy community finds the 'compassionate listening ear' approach to be totally inadequate, I make absolutely no apology, because the overwhelming data from clients confirms a refusal to concede a relationship of equality based on truthful answers to questions in the context of personal spiritual searching. The frightening and tragic result is that the pastoral care offered by churches and their formulations of basic tenets of faith have been *causal factors* in the process leading to infection in the clients in my care.

To make my case, I would like to take a brief 'backward' glance, if I may, at the historical and theological background to the story.

The response of the Church to HIV has been determined by three main issues.

- First, the fact that most of the people initially diagnosed were from 'marginal' backgrounds, very often associated with what the Church thought of as 'immoral' life styles: gay people, sex workers, drug users and the like.
- Second, the fear of, the indifference to or the plain ignorance about the needs of peripheral groups on the part of the institutional Church and most of its leaders and members.
- Third, the grim reality of the situation – HIV was diagnosed when it had progressed to AIDS, and the only possible outcome was death.

Those who led the initial response employed language and imagery from the Christian tradition that they believed would help sufferers feel incorporated, forgiven and accepted into the Church despite having been seen to be at odds with it morally. That position served to motivate the wider Church community to action and to an appropriation of the issues of the 'marginal' into the mainstream. The dynamics of the language employed were that the community should be more aware of its self-identity as the active presence of Christ in the world, and act accordingly by incorporating the marginal within the mainstream community.

The language was therefore dominated by terms such as compassion, forgiveness, marginality and the love of God. The message that 'God loves you no matter who and what you are' was seen as definitely helpful to those facing stigma and death, and the Gospel images used were Jesus' inclusion of sinners, prostitutes and tax collectors. The healing of lepers was a favourite. Indeed, the first thing I ever read on the subject of HIV was a small booklet that had an image on the cover of Jesus' mother holding her dead son (who was covered in Kaposi sarcoma lesions) at the foot of the cross.

While this response was the one that the then current theology dictated, the context has changed dramatically. The advent of combination therapy means, to put it very bluntly, *the solution has become the problem.*

This is clear from the stories of my clients. All of the people in the care of the chaplaincy have suffered what they describe as 'disillusionment', 'despair' or 'depression' caused by or deeply connected to the failure of their faith communities to handle fundamental issues of sexuality and gender in an intelligent way.

Part 2: The stories of my clients

By closing the shutters on the various and multiple attempts of clients to describe their own experiences in their own terms and to give them cogent answers, the different churches contributed to the journey to infection of both heterosexual women and gay men.

The majority of my clients fell into these two categories:

- heterosexual African women (usually married)
- gay white men.

On the surface at least, these two groups seem to have very little in common with each other, except, of course, that they are HIV positive. However, any period of time spent with them soon throws up the factor that they do have in common: the terrible impact of the Church on their lives.

Cases of African women

All of the women in the chaplaincy's care who fall into this category expressed deep resentment towards faith communities (pastors, priests and leaders, in particular) for not providing empowering advice prior to their infection.

The majority of cases originated in neo-Pentecostalist or Evangelical churches. The major issue with every single one of them was the self-empowerment of the woman in deciding how to deal with a possibly unfaithful and infected husband.

The need of these women to hear self-empowering advice about taking control of the situation and asserting themselves outside socially assigned gender roles was vital. Yet the answers offered to them revolved around a 'wife being subservient to her husband' or 'God having created women as under the authority of men'. The majority of the women concerned faced outright hostility and accusations of being 'led astray by the devil' or of 'Western godlessness' when they suggested their right to assert themselves in the home and very specifically in the context of sexual relationships.

In a smaller number of cases (those who belonged to Roman Catholic or Episcopal churches), the issue was that condoms were 'sinful'. Alternatively, in a few cases, the assertion was made that condoms help to spread or cause HIV infection.

All the women under the care of the chaplaincy had sought advice about the possibility of infection before they were diagnosed. All were discouraged by faith-based advice from taking preventative action.

Cases of gay white men

In the cases of the gay white men in the care of the chaplaincy, the dynamics of the contributory issues took a different form. (I must clarify here that there are a number of self-identified bisexual and gay African men in the care of the chaplaincy as well, but I want to discuss generality at the moment.)

All these clients spoke of repeated attempts to find help to account for and to cope with the genesis of their sexuality. Their universal experience was that they did not have a choice in their orientation. Most often their search for help was met by the dogmatic assertion of traditional values, stigmatization and accusation. They experienced direct confrontation and rebuke as well as gentle assertion of these perspectives.

Many Roman Catholic clients had had imputed on to them the motivation that they were 'deliberately rebelling against God', and those from more 'Bible-based' faith communities faced the accusation of 'satanic obsession' or 'possession'. More than 75 per cent of clients were faced with advice that relied on the creation stories from the book of Genesis to assert traditional sexual norms.

Every single client (even those who sought advice from more 'liberal' clergy) spoke of the experience of being 'left dangling' when it came to the issues of sexuality in relation to God and the Church. They often felt the weight of expectation to retreat into a private world with their 'own answers'. Clear understanding of their situation, thoughtful discussion of their questions, support and critique of churches' traditional reactions to questions about sexuality were not in any way forthcoming. All clients were left with a sense of shame and secrecy.

One client described the feeling as 'banging my head against a brick wall', and a great many described the physical sensation that accompanied these dealings as akin to 'being suffocated'.

In nearly all cases, clients reported strong feelings of despondency and depression as a result of their encounters with the Church. All were honest enough to connect these feelings to behaviours that were frankly either secretive and therefore unsafe, or explicitly self-destructive. They were 'acting out' the roles they had been assigned. All these behaviours had the same end result: *infection*.

I hope I have at least established the *possibility* of a link between the failure of faith communities to build a relationship based on intelligent questioning and the causes (contributory or direct) of HIV infection. Despair, disconnection and low self-esteem all significantly increase the risk of infection. The rhetoric of the faith community would save us from all of those, but the practice of those in leadership or offering pastoral care often increases despair and lowers self-esteem.

Consequences for spirit and body

I want to go on now to look at some of the other contributing or 'subsidiary' issues that have kept the chaplaincy's clients in a cul-de-sac of despair, self-hatred and frustration.

1 The prohibition of 'negative' emotions

In every single client, frustration as a result of the unwillingness or inability on the part of the representative of the faith community to explore their issues in a reasoned and open way contributed to heightened aggression and even in some cases to what can only be described as 'fury'. The pastoral or spiritual care reportedly offered to clients suffocated them with repression. They were not given help or permission to analyse and contextualize their feelings and questions. The images used to justify this prohibition displayed the sort of holiness and wholeness that demanded dispassion and disconnection from confusion, grief, anger and frustration.

2 Physical manifestations of frustration

All our clients described experiencing, at one point or another, behaviour induced by anxiety and frustration. The most common were drug or alcohol addiction followed by one that particularly interested me: eating disorders. These took the form of overeating or comfort eating, but also, in a surprisingly large number, anorexia and bulimia.

Again, help from faith communities proved to be utterly inadequate, with a complete failure to make connections between embodiment and the frustrations connected to the search for spiritual and emotional answers. Any advice invariably separated 'body' and 'soul'. In the great majority of cases, abstinence or asceticism was recommended as a spiritual 'cure'. A small number of cases resulted in the laying on of hands for healing or for exorcism.

In every single case, the faith story of the individual was neglected.

The spiritual and pastoral approaches employed in the attempted care of clients were not only inadequate but also damaging. The end result was a bifurcation between the subject and the content of their experience. The imposition of a 'universal' theological narrative (be it scriptural or ecclesial) contributed to clients reducing their self-definition to issues that were stigmatized or inadequately treated.

All clients, trustfully seeking guidance from the Church, were led immediately to define themselves excessively in terms of gender and sexuality – and therefore with HIV status – to the exclusion of any other personal characteristics. All clients were unable to relate to or appreciate what were (to others) their own very conspicuous qualities, such as intelligence, concentration, kindness or empathy. By accepting the pastoral stereotype, they lost the ability to value themselves.

They exhibited an inability to distance themselves from abusive personal relationships because of their need for approval in the face of feelings of self-loathing. A significant number reported a lack of motivation in the workplace. It would not be inaccurate, in my opinion, to speak of an 'ossification' or a blockage in personal development caused by the spiritual images pressed on them and the nature of the care they received. This was most notably demonstrated by the resulting inability to evaluate and reflect on their sexuality and gender in ways that would help them successfully integrate their personalities. Their identities were lost, and new identities conforming to traditional spiritual stereotypes had been forced on them.

The Church's response to HIV

This initial reflection on the experience of clients in their specific faith and life contexts leaves us in no doubt about the seriousness of the challenge their testimonies represent. It both enables and forces us to view aspects of the wider response of the Church to HIV.

The great majority of clients view the Church's response to HIV with deep sadness. Their overwhelming impression is that churches have 'appropriated' the HIV issue to justify and fortify the authority of their own moral teaching.

Many also reported that they felt 'used' by their church; one client even described feeling like a 'ping-pong ball' in their church's internal and external conflicts.

On the basis of such evidence, I would suggest that, having failed to do self-critical analysis about the development of gender issues and sexuality in the context of their spiritual care, churches have rushed in with oversimplified and stereotypical analysis of the causes of HIV infection. Many clients felt very angry that explanations seemed to be concerned only with 'the bigger picture', and their own personal stories were ignored in order to make general points. One client referred to this as 'almost entirely self-serving, shallow and inaccurate'.

A clear example of this would be the pattern of blaming homosexuality, promiscuity and (by some) 'Western godless secularism' as

the source of infection. In some extreme forms, it becomes ammuni-
tion with which to attack liberal elements on moral and theological
grounds in a church's own internecine strife.

In such a climate, the issues raised in examining the spiritual care
of clients seem further justified by even a cursory reading of official
pronouncements on HIV by church hierarchies. Again and again, the
spiritual contributory causes of behaviour remain unanalysed. No
connection, or at best very little, is made to basic theological themes
as presented in pastoral contexts experienced by most 'ordinary'
believers, such as African churches declaiming homosexuality as a
'Western' phenomenon of a piece with exploitative economic models.
Those of us who are HIV positive (remember it doesn't exist apart
from those who actually live with it!) are left feeling that we are mere
'cannon fodder'. Generalities feed the controversy but miss the person. The clients become peripheral casualties to those engaged in the
ecclesial phoney war.

One feeling common to all the people I work with (and to myself,
by the way) is that the Church's attitudes suggest that the causes of
HIV are always somebody else's fault – in particular the client's –
while the response is always the Church's private property. In prep-
arations for the Pope's visit to the UK in September 2010, it was
suggested that 'the Church understands HIV since it provides most
of the care' and, more recently, 'no one does more in regard to HIV
than the Church'.[1] Such attitudes have the effect of precluding a thor-
ough investigation of the Church's contribution to infection rates, or
a radical criticism of its basic faith-based propositions. In effect, it is
saying that the Church 'owns' HIV as its own private constituency.
What is not explored is the lack of a speedy response on the part of
the Church in the beginning, nor that many of the major personalities who led the way in changing public opinion were explicitly not
from the Church. In other words, Princess Diana got there before the
faith communities!

Using such tactics, the Church exempts itself from responsibility
and criticism. A particularly appalling example of this attitude is an
incident that affected several of my African clients. A West African
Roman Catholic prelate was quoted as saying, 'I touch people with

---

[1] Heard on a television programme covering the Pope's visit to Ireland.

HIV every single day. I know this problem. What do Western liberal theologians know? Have they ever even met a person with HIV?'

In case I should be viewed as in any way partisan, however, liberal as well as conservative church leaders seem to excel at moralizing HIV in an unthinking manner. This issue is felt deeply by every client in my care, and it focuses on the question of the application of the ideas of 'compassion' and the 'love of God' in response to HIV. Far too many theological and spiritual responses to HIV take refuge in a trite rolling out of what are perceived as the appropriate, standard gospel images – 'whores, tax collectors and lepers'. These gospel images are deployed in a truly unthinking way as the basis of the Church's response to HIV. It is an approach that uses the language of acceptance and compassion but does so in a way that humiliates, violates and even exploits the clients.

A prominent female bishop of the Anglican Communion dealing with the issues of inclusion of 'marginal groups', including HIV sufferers, talked about her former diocese where even people who ran brothels were included and encouraged to come to church. The most negative response – although it is reflective of all responses to these images – was from a female client: 'I am not a f****** whore' were her exact words! Again, a prominent gay bishop preached about inclusion by telling a congregation in London, 'God loves you no matter what you are. God doesn't make garbage but he does collect it.'

Every single client I work with feels disempowered, humiliated and made more vulnerable by such images. They are not a means of caring for or valuing people who already freely admit to feelings of low self-worth, low self-esteem and moral stigmatization. Whatever the correctness or otherwise of these biblical images and their interpretation, their deployment in such ways has terrible effects on the people they are supposed to help. How are they relevant to those with HIV who are plague victims or rape victims who didn't fight back?

The irresistible conviction that has grown in me since I began this work is a fearful one. It is possible to read the data as showing that the Church is creating victims and then feeding off their misery in order to justify itself and its moral and spiritual authority. I have given these presentations various titles. Three linger with me because of the challenges they raise. The first is 'The terrorism of compassion', which I used to attempt to call attention graphically to the data demonstrating the failure of pastoral methods. The second title develops that thought – 'The solution becomes the problem' – and opened up the question of the Church's collusion and culpability in the process. The third title is 'Wisdom and the love of God', which is less directly confrontational but evokes the spirit of the Wisdom Literature of the Hebrew Scriptures where, in the fierce heat of contextual engagement in theological debate, the character of God's love is refined.

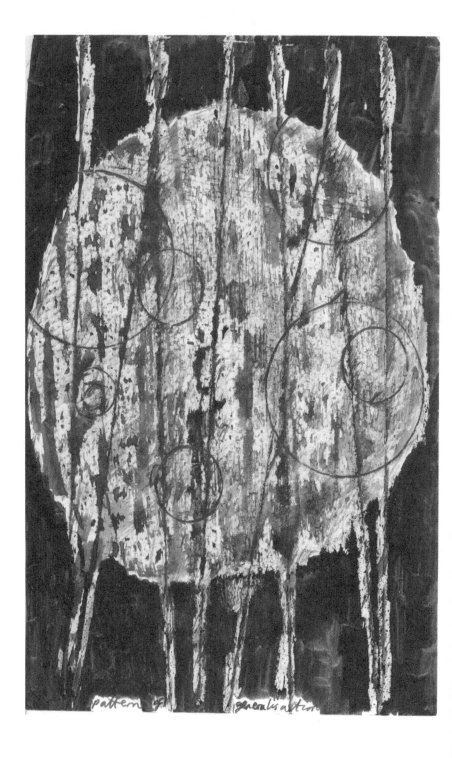

pattern of   generalisation

Sixth testimony
The chaplain's testimony

At this point the testimony moves from what has been a disciplined articulation of the voices of the clients to the way in which the chaplain has wrestled more personally with the issues raised as he has engaged with them. We begin with an introduction to his work, written by the Revd Steve Penrose:

> Our chaplain was appointed in 2008 to work with individual people living with HIV and who were searching for some meaning to their lives. He is the first full-time chaplain; he succeeded someone who was employed only part-time. His commitment to clients has meant that the workload has grown during that time from almost no clients to in excess of 360 at any one time. He has developed a way of listening to clients that blocks out any preconceived ideas and thoughts so he can concentrate on what the clients actually say. Most of us only hear the first few words or sentences that come our way and they trigger in us a thought process so we do not hear the rest of the story. But when the chaplain feeds back to clients what he has heard, clients feel that for the first time someone has fully heard their story. He has discovered by listening to clients how they have suffered through the abuse they have received from members of their various communities, including their faith communities.
>
> The chaplain's commitment to what he has learnt from listening to the clients has compelled him to share that learning with the faith communities. However, this has not been easy for him, as most faith communities believe they have all the answers. Therefore, on numerous occasions, they have become abusive to the chaplain. He has received from faith communities the same treatment as the clients themselves. This has not stopped him from continuing to get the London HIV Chaplaincy message across. He sticks to his commitment to the clients through thick and thin.

The chaplain talks about his own journey in a personal, contextual and theological response

I went into this work with no clients and I was filled with as many preconceptions about HIV care as you can imagine. I had been very influenced by an approach similar to the 'marginal Jew' approach to Jesus in his first-century context, and basically entered into work that was shaped by that message and centred on all the usual clichés about compassion and 'healing lepers and outcasts'. I made the presumption that the major issue pastorally and theologically was that people needed to know that 'God loves them no matter what'.

What I learned in the first three years reshaped my life. I was driven to fierce criticism of much of the theology and pastoral care provided by the Church. The encounters with my clients – facing their courage, intelligence, anger and stubborn determination to remain people of authentic faith – have both challenged me and shaped (and continue to shape) my theological response. My experiences have quite literally changed my life.

I was forced to move from offering clients 'a listening ear', very much along the standard pastoral care lines, to a radically different approach. The active images the chaplaincy now uses to describe its work with its diverse range of clients are predominantly about *providing a time in which to relate*. I choose these words deliberately above the standard 'place to listen' because our purpose very clearly became about *not* encouraging dependent victims to take refuge in our service, *but about encountering, responding and learning from the stories shared*. In this way, the clients, the churches and I grow in a more mature way by relating through the process of engagement.

I discovered that the Church has everything to learn from the stories of those who have sought care as they live with HIV. At that point, however, I met real resistance to such a message. It came from two directions. The first was from those who believe it is the Church's job simply to repeat eternal verities to 'sinners' – not to learn from them and be reshaped by their sharing. The second was from an organizational direction that called into question the nature of the chaplaincy itself. This view held that client numbers were of ultimate importance, and the spiritual life was merely about offering comfort. This was the conviction of the London Ecumenical Aids Trust, the umbrella organization with which the chaplaincy had worked up until that point. The two views had this in common: the operative paradigm was a one-way street in which the client was effectively robbed of a voice, and the chaplaincy can take credit for looking after the vulnerable.

In the face of these views, long held, theologically deeply founded, practical and widely accepted, I had the terrifying experience of hearing the simple story offered by all my clients. I hope it makes you as uncomfortable as it made me as I encountered it again and again: *that the pastoral care they received at the hands of their various churches* prior *to diagnosis contributed in significant ways to their infection.*

The crux of the matter with all clients was this: when they approached their respective pastors or priests about the issue of either gender or sexuality, they were not given an authentic opportunity to enter into a dialogical relationship. If you think I am about to attack conservative churches that reduce women to servile objects and sexuality to a heterosexual married preserve, you are correct, but only partly so! There were just as many clients who complained about the more 'liberal' approach, which consisted of platitudes such as, 'Don't worry, God loves you; don't think about it; don't worry about it,' and robbed them of their motivation to wrestle with the central questions of their being.

Both approaches shared the refusal to air fundamental questions openly and critically. Both denied clients opportunities to argue, attack, search for answers and find ways to assimilate their identities, criticize and evaluate how they identified themselves as individual human beings of value and so develop a sense of self wider than gender or sexuality. By failing to provide this time and this sort of engagement, by the time I met the clients they were all identifying themselves principally and excessively as 'women', 'gays' and 'HIV positive', to the extent of missing out a vast array of other impressive qualities, such as intelligence, courage, tenacity and faithfulness, which were all immediately obvious to me.

Their stories were desperately similar. In the face of the initial frustration at being unable to enter into any sort of real relationship in their pastoral encounters with faith leaders, they all reported reactive behaviour such as fury, mood swings, substance abuse and self-destructive patterns of behaviour that would be considered as both 'acting out' their perceived role and self-victimizing. These behaviours included eating disorders, promiscuity, entering or colluding with co-dependent relationships, and an inability to achieve or succeed in work or friendships – all the direct result of an excessive negative self-image.

As if this were not enough, the clients' experience of care received following their HIV positive diagnosis was devastating. All reported having immorality imputed to them as a reason for their predicament. The responsibility was shifted to them as sinners. The fact of them having been 'sinned against' was never considered. Inevitably, the images used to locate them were 'leprosy', 'healing' and 'Jesus among sinners, tax collectors and prostitutes'. They were linked with the then current examples of 'madams' who ran Nevada brothels, or the 'rubbish' that God doesn't make but collects. These are both examples from well-known liberal bishops: one gay, the other a woman. Both should have known better.

'If God does not love me as I am, God does not love me!' Doing theology together

Again and again, the main theological issue my clients and I have had to face together is, what do we actually mean by the phrase 'God loves you'?

I have already noted that if God loves you *despite who you are*, then in actual fact God doesn't love you, because God doesn't take you seriously in any way but rather sweeps your issues, difficulties and problems under the carpet.

Ideas have consequences. If we perceive God as modelling love 'despite who we are', then we don't get to love ourselves. If love is described to us as a one-way street, that is how we will practise it! Our theology has anthropological implications.

I have tried repeatedly to explore this issue. The response of one professional theologian was to comment that this was not unknown even in Scripture and to proceed to quote St Paul: 'where sin increased, grace abounded all the more' (Romans 5.20). Paul's point was that some early Christians attempted to justify immoral behaviour by using the excuse that the more they sinned, the more God's forgiveness would then be forthcoming. This misses the point in a way that is entirely characteristic of the Church's response to HIV. I was *not* dealing with people shaped by their own deliberate sin. The dynamics of everything I have been trying to describe are completely the other way round. I was dealing with the 'sinned against'. Most of the spiritual care my clients have received consisted of being told that it is only when you are totally pathetic and vulnerable that you are in fact worthy of love and attention. As soon as you demonstrate intelligence, strength, determination and anger, or you question anything, then you become totally unlovable and offensive to God and the Church, resisting God's love and not accepting your own sin.

By using a theological structure that does not take seriously a truly covenantal relationship that works two ways – between God and the individual and between God and the Church and is as a result explicitly dialogical from *both* sides – the contents of subjective experience have been repressed or denied as a means to learn and grow. This is true *both* for the Church and for the individuals concerned.

The theological care of my clients has been totally separated from its contextual matrix and is therefore utterly useless at best, and at worst is maiming those it is supposed to help.

My clients and their impact on me forced me to become increasingly concerned about what might be termed 'virtue' or 'character' and the character that is formed in those we are sent to care for by the theological language we use. I remain utterly convinced that while love is a fundamental human need and compassion is a required expression of a life of faith, we have to use much more wisdom in analysing what those words mean and how we use them. It simply isn't enough to bandy about the words 'love' and 'compassion' and be satisfied that we have applied the panacea to all wounds.

This theological and pastoral pilgrimage led to three areas that I needed to look at again.

- What does it mean to say that God is 'loving'?
- What is meant by a loving, covenantal response to God from us as human beings? What personal characteristics should it be developing?
- What responsibilities are implied and what are the dynamics involved when churches use the terms 'love' and 'compassion'?

For me, if this process of searching was to be radical in its truest sense, the questions needed to be asked in the particular context of each personal situation and then set in the wider context of a relational covenant that affirms all parties. I began to discover an excellent framework of authentic 'covenantal' theology in the examples of Abraham, Jacob, Moses and Esther. They set an example that is affirmed by God and is very far from passive or supinely obedient. They point towards lessons I have tried to learn more recently from Holocaust theology, which embodies the Hebrew tradition of arguing with God.

If the love of God does not allow such an honest response to flourish, it is not love. It is as simple as that.

I recognize that my experience and work is only one small piece in the necessary dialogue of contemporary theology. But from the small context of a marginal people in a marginal place, our faith began. The memory of that dynamic needs to be at the heart of responsible theology and pastoral care. This is the consequence of my calling: to feed the experiences of my clients into a wider forum of theological reflection, training, preaching, care and witness in the lives of churches. We can confirm that HIV is still as much a pressing issue for churches as ever. It is my conviction that this is a proper theological concern, and the challenges and insights it brings offer healing and new direction to the whole community of faith.

isolated symptoms

Seventh testimony
'The love of neighbour: dynamics of HIV reflection'

The chaplain originally wrote this article for The Epworth Review. *It was published in 2010 and offers his initial reflections on his role as chaplain and his responses to the particular challenges posed to contributors by* The Epworth Review's *editor, the late and respected Revd Angela Shier-Jones.*

The purpose of this article is to take a highly personal and alternative look at the purpose behind those theological reflections and statements concerning HIV that make their way into non-specialist publications. The material often ends up being circulated among those people most affected by the virus who are seeking to make personal and spiritual sense of what is happening to them. Such material is therefore highly influential, even though it is seldom either academic or particularly accurate.

The people I work with have only one thing in common: they live in or in the vicinity of London; otherwise they are very diverse. They are gay and straight, black and white, young and old, male and female; they have been infected by unfaithful husbands or lovers; they have been cavalier or sensible; they have been courageous or they have fallen apart in the face of their diagnosis.

The point of this article is not to deny the virtue in reflecting on such aspects as the abuse of women, the moral irresponsibility of adulterous partners or promiscuous singles, or even the need for moral restraint or for spiritual guidelines. Such reflections have informed a great deal of literature that has been available in the past concerning HIV. It is my intention instead to consider the effect that certain theological images have had, and continue to have, on people who are HIV positive at a much more subliminal or discrete level. It is also my intention to draw out the, hopefully unintentional, effect of these images with regard to the role and self-image of the Church.

The fundamental theological concepts with which this paper wrestles are not very complex. They focus on the commandments of Christ to 'love thy neighbour as thyself', and to 'lay down your life for your friends'(Matthew 22.39; John 15.13, paraphrased). It is perhaps about time that such 'simple' tenets were brought to the forefront of the Church's reflections about itself as an institution and its role. This might prove more informative and creative than a reflection on how the Church imparts its wisdom to those it perhaps sees (or certainly gives the impression it sees) as the objects of its care.

The day I was diagnosed HIV positive stands out in my mind for one thing above all: namely the way I deployed the theological tradition I had inherited. To the young and rather overawed doctor I behaved exactly as was expected of me: calm and (in her words) 'serene'. I reflected with her on the fact that throughout my priestly life I had preached the marginal Christ. But as soon as she left the room I turned to my best friend, who is a priest, and said, 'Oh my God, I am a *leper!*' and I started to cry.

I meant both kinds of reaction. I had focused on Jesus, the marginal Jew, in all my preaching as an antidote to the triumphalist and institutionalized Christ who featured in so many Sunday sermons. Therefore I naturally turned to that tradition for strength when faced with the difficulty I now had to endure. What shocked me was that this image of Christ afforded me neither comfort nor consolation; it didn't strengthen or help me. It made me feel worse! I found myself in a place spiritually where I was hearing the voice of judgement, not only from the Church (already well practised at giving that out!) but also from myself. I was inadvertently, habitually, using theological and scriptural images to add weight to my own shoulders and to blame myself for my stupidity, immorality and scandal.

In the days and years since then, those same images have been deployed more or less as a stock-in-trade for well-meaning (or otherwise) reflections on HIV. The words 'marginal', 'stigmatized', 'leper' and 'outcast' figure fairly prominently in a great many articles and proposals for courses designed to educate the laity and the clergy about HIV, almost all of which are well intentioned. They are used by those wanting to advocate a more open and inclusive approach to people who are HIV positive in the life of the Church; very often those same courses and articles are dismissive and angry with those who stigmatize those of us who are HIV positive.

Such reflections tend to dwell on the importance of 'not judging' the individual, usually with the proviso that 'only God knows'. As a priest, for example, I was asked if I had contracted the virus 'innocently' (meaning that I had not had sex or been raped or that, at a push, I had had sex before ordination). I was very conscious of the fact that if it became obvious that I had indeed contracted the virus sexually, and with a man(!), then the 'only God can judge' stance would be adopted.

My personal experience has been that, in most cases, the content of Christian reflections on HIV is (very often without trying to be) moralistic, judgemental and patronizing. But such reflections needn't have bothered; I was ahead of them every single time. I blamed myself and apologized to God and thought of myself as a leper whose only way to holiness was to drink the cup of being an outcast to the dregs, in order to be like Jesus; to find the key to my own self-worth by reflecting that Jesus was 'unclean' (or was treated as such) and so my way to redemption was to revel in this status. Finally I took refuge – and I am not alone in this, I assure you – in the well-attested belief that, in the end, Jesus actually took the status of the sinful in order to take away our sins.

I have now lived knowingly with the virus for three years and have spent almost the same amount of time working with others in the same position. What has struck me repeatedly during this time has been the inadequacy of most of the theological reflection done on our behalf (and even on occasions by ourselves). Many of the images offered never go beyond the sheer negatives, whether they have scriptural backing or not, and when they do they tend to be rejected for the wrong reasons. For example, the image of Jesus relating to lepers is the most commonly used theological motif for the way in which the Church should relate to those who have HIV. This image, however, ends up being rejected on at least two fronts: first, because, medically speaking, the two complaints are so radically different; and second, because the moral issues pertaining to each have so little (if anything) in common.

The real failure of the image, however, lies in its insistence that a person's spiritual state is inextricably linked to his or her medical state. Why? I mean, frankly, please: why? Would the same type of link be at all acceptable in the case of diabetes, even though that condition can be caused by a lifetime of overindulgence, or in the case of cancer, with all the evidence that we now have about the relationship between some cancers and lifestyle choices? Or would it be acceptable to link another condition I also suffer from – epilepsy – to my spiritual state? Even if it were possible and/or acceptable, the Church is understandably reluctant to make such associations, perhaps because it knows that it would be unlikely to avoid censure and ridicule if it did?

The most fundamental question for someone with HIV is not medical or even explicitly theological, but profoundly ontological. Can, or rather should, a person's spiritual existence, their state before God, be defined almost totally by his or her medical condition? Surely defining a person's spiritual state according to the need for physical healing or the state of well-being sets all of humanity on a collision course with unrighteousness? It mocks the Church's proclamation of the optimism of grace and of the ability to enter into a lifelong loving relationship with God through Christ, for all humans eventually fall sick and die, if not from AIDS then from something else.

To borrow the words of the editor of this journal at a meeting of the contributors, 'If meeting God was such a good thing, then why are we doing everything in our power to stop people doing it?!' By referring to this I do not mean to imply that people should be denied treatment for an illness, only to highlight the ill-thought-through theology and dynamics that seem to underline much of the Church's reflection on this matter. It simply will not do to imply that people who are HIV positive can only use the model of the healing of the leper as a fundamental reference point in their reflections around their relationship with the person of Jesus.

Neither is it helpful for the Church constantly to dwell on sexual behaviour even when it is trying to be more inclusive, or on embodiedness and physicality. This often masks the much more important connection between social and economic exclusion and HIV, including gender. This is most evident in the battle against HIV in the developing world. There, women and men struggle to obtain treatment because the drug companies keep the prices high. Women have to travel for miles to clinics to obtain treatment; children are left orphaned or abandoned. The wealthy parts of the world are played off against the poor regions, and the rich within one society are treated at the cost of the poor.

In the point I am seeking to make, I am not trying to avoid the fact that certain groups are more at risk of infection than others.

I am a gay man who feels much abused at the hands of organized Christianity, but that does not mean I am looking to deny the need for theological reflection on sexual behaviour and Christian responsibility. I would be the last person to ignore the issues that arise in the economic arena, especially when it comes to the way in which that affects the life expectancy of someone with HIV and their ability to access antiretrovirals. I do not deny the legitimacy of such reflection. But we need to ask why the Church in particular has chosen to focus on these issues rather than on what it means to be human and to be HIV positive.

I agree with the editor of this journal who challenged a theologian from South Africa and his talk on the importance of doing work on these issues by asking why similar efforts were not being made to tackle other 'economic' diseases. Why are the actions and reflections of the Church around the issues of HIV so important? From my own experience and reflections, I am led to conclude that they might be one of many means by which the Church looks to attract attention to itself and, in particular, to establish a role for itself in society that will be recognized by the policymakers and lawmakers. The actions of the Church throughout the world, but especially in the developing world, certainly lead to grants being given and clinics being set up around church centres. This in turn enables the Church to draw to itself the very weakest and to work to convince them of their need to belong to the Church; only within the boundaries of the Church will they (we) be given the crutch they need to limp through what remains of their lives. We poor marginal beings, so desperately in need of forgiveness, will receive what we need from the Church . . . and all this while the Church is able to do what a recently appointed Roman Catholic Archbishop called 'setting the moral agenda'.

So let's be clear what may be happening – as hard as it may be to hear it: *those of us who are HIV positive are often, indeed very often, fed disempowering images that concentrate on our personal weaknesses. This can result in defining us totally by our medical conditions or gender or earning ability. These images are then used to 'hook' us into the Church, either discretely or otherwise. We are told that we weak or displaced individuals will be welcome in the Church, and that the Church is better than wider society because it alone can see beyond the label of diseased, sick, leprous. This seems to be especially true of the more 'liberal' churches, which still give the impression that their willingness to include us and look beyond our sexuality, gender or illness or lack of earning power is a virtue on their part.*

Yet, as I have already noted, all human beings will get sick, will grow old and will die. All human beings have some kind of sexual orientation. All human beings have to provide for their needs in some way. There is nothing unique in any of those conditions. We who are HIV positive are no more defined by them than anyone else is; they are part of the human condition. Yet the fundamental content of most Church reflections surrounding HIV still seeks to highlight the difference in these areas between those who are HIV positive and those who are not. Worse, they then tend to make a virtue out of the acceptance of sufferers, which is somehow different from the acceptance of everyone else. Including and embracing those who are damaged and feeling excluded, however, isn't an act of virtue on the part of the Church; particularly not when, as may well have been the case, it has been the Church's own teaching that helped in part to create the social and personal alienation being experienced in the first place. The Church has played its part in the debates surrounding homosexuality, gender and economic independence and the control of productive technology. It cannot claim to be innocent in the spread and development of the very conditions that it now subverts in order to draw the poor and wretched to itself. Above all, the question must be asked, 'Where, in all of this, are we who are invited in, empowered or directed beyond the very limitations and issues that screwed us up in the first place?'

I realize that this is not an easy essay to read, and I could be accused of cynicism in the extreme, but this has been the personal experience of the Church of both me and people like me with HIV. A good deal of the Church's public reflection on HIV appears to be used as a springboard to pontificate to a society that has largely rejected the Church's message that it is the answer to society's ills. Society would not have got into this mess if it had listened to the Church. The Church alone, it is suggested, sees clearly the moral relativity that breeds the spread of such morally implicative diseases. The suffering and pain of the very group of people for whom the Church proclaims its compassion can appear to that same group of people to be mercilessly exploited as a means of justifying the Church having a moral voice – but that is just another term for power or influence.

It can seem as though the images used in Church reflections and statements on the nature of what it is to be human are deployed in a very particular way. When Jesus is offered as the epitome of what it means to be a perfect human, the image of Christ is usually confined to that of a self-sacrificing moral teacher who, while keeping company with the morally tainted, pays attention to them only in so far as they swell the ranks of his disciples. This creates the illusion that the real work of Christ was not to make disciples but to attack the general moral condition of society and pontificate about his own vital status. The fact that the actions of Jesus were considered immoral by many who did not believe in a division between morals and rituals tends not to be mentioned or developed in any way. Similarly, popular accessible theological discussion often ignores or marginalizes the very real and personal sense of empowerment that Jesus gave to his disciples, which freed these so-called undesirable individuals from social and religious disapproval.

Perhaps, more importantly, there is frequently a complete lack of consideration of the full humanity that Jesus displayed: of his anger and fear, his physical ordinariness or frustration with the disciples when they couldn't get the point of his message. References to the more mundane aspects of Jesus are often explained away as 'concessions' to our weakness or as misperceptions of the real situation. Images of Jesus partying and laughing and keeping company are very seldom used.

The end result of this is that the language and images used when the Church reflects on HIV tend to restrict or inhibit the spiritual and psychological responses of those for whom they were designed by disempowering them: it would appear that the only self-images that are permissible are victim or guest at a pity party, someone who is tolerated while the Church goes about the real business of challenging society for the very moral defects that many of these victims are portrayed as holding. The message given to those of us with HIV appears to be, 'You are in, but not really welcome.' Only Jesus is perfect enough to know that tax collectors and sinners can be incorporated. Ultimately, for the sufferer, the only permitted response to the Church-mediated encounter with Christ is to be even more repressed and self-hating than you were before.

However, my experience teaches me that this is not the truth. The encounter with the human Jesus very often unleashes the emotional, intellectual and, yes, passionate side of those of us who encounter him through the experience of HIV. The humanity of Jesus is the powder keg that releases the gamut of our own humanity, releasing within us a new world that brings doubt and fear. It is empowering and potentially chaotic. It is energetic and active. It awakens us beyond sweet demure smiles and needs channelling beyond loneliness and ostracism. But the Church isn't, or doesn't seem, able to provide a nurturing environment where this empowerment can find a home. Instead, the conditions of acceptance are to continue to admit our deficiency and to cheer on an institution that feeds off our misfortunes like a vampire. When I challenged a bishop, who shall remain nameless, about this theological abuse ('abuse' because it sets people in a double bind), I was informed that I didn't understand. The survival of the Church was more important to society than the troubles of a group of unfortunates who, in any case, would receive their reward in heaven.

My purpose in raising these issues has not been to canonize those of us who are HIV positive any more than it is to demonize the Church. It is quite simply a plea for reflections or articles on this matter to be centred on people rather than on 'issues'. People with HIV do not want to remain with one hand tied behind their backs all their lives. Nor do they want to adopt a persona of a wounded, pathetic individual as the only way to survive and thrive. To be truly alive, to have lived life in all its fullness: the promise of Christ is to be empowered not by permission but at our deepest level, the level of what is authentically human. The fundamental reflection about HIV should not be ecclesial or soteriological, not social or medical, but human. It should be centred around the humanity Jesus portrayed, not as a cardboard cutout to be 'imitated' (what a hideous concept), but as a person to be encountered and to whom we respond.

I have already mentioned the question posed by the editor of this journal at a meeting, when she challenged us to justify why the Church does, and should, put so much energy and effort into the issues surrounding HIV and not into other medical or social issues. My answer is simple. In my opinion, the Church often uses these issues to bolster its own life. Whether deliberately or not, it sees those of us who are weakened and afraid because of HIV as a lucrative conversion target, just as the platform of HIV is a way of increasing its own power. This is aside from the responsibility that the Church has in the very areas touched on in any dialogue about HIV.

As history will undoubtedly recount, the Church has been very much part of the problem – unwittingly perhaps, but it has nonetheless contributed to the disempowerment and self-hatred among individuals as well as to the societal attitudes that have helped fan the flames of this pandemic. What it has done is worked with the very fundamental teaching of its founder: love your neighbour as yourself; lay down your life for your friends. Whether intentional or not, it has tended to talk *about*, rather than *to* people with HIV and acted as though their status before God, unlike that of every other human being, is directly related to, if not dictated by, their medical condition. The Church has spiritualized the commandments of Christ until they are deemed to be good advice for anyone except itself as an institution, and it has seen the complexity of its words as a sign of its sophistication.

The Church has been a part of the problem. The dynamics of reflection on HIV are self-obsessed and damaging for those it claims to wish to help. The question remains: can the Church also be part of the solution?

terrorism of compassion

Eighth testimony
The cost of testimony – a theological encounter

This piece is short but nevertheless central to the task of theological reflection raised by the chaplaincy. In November 2011, in an examination of Genesis 29 and part of the synagogue liturgy, the chaplain explored the nature of the covenantal relationship that is central to the chaplaincy's work with a small group of Methodist leaders who gathered regularly to reflect on theological issues. On the basis of his work as chaplain to the London HIV community, attached to the Centre for Contextual Theology and dealing with 300 clients, his role was to be a resource for churches to stimulate theological reflection arising from paying attention to the very specific context in which he works and the issues generated by the clients with whom he engages.

After describing his work, the chaplain explored with the group the theological and pastoral approach that had changed the nature of the chaplaincy from one in which a 'holding hands' model with passive clients was the operative mode, through significant struggle, to a much more dynamic relationship based on the understanding of covenant. The nature of the covenantal relationship as found in the Hebrew Scriptures became the key to understanding the new approach of the chaplaincy. It is modelled in the stories of the way in which the patriarchs and Moses engaged with God and is reflected in the threefold synagogue liturgy that had its origins in the Second Temple.

He drew a stark and uncomfortable contrast between the following two most prevalent theological metaphors used in HIV care.

- 'God loves you; it doesn't matter who or what you are', which is based on Jesus' actions of healing the lepers and the sick, making the deaf hear and the dumb speak, and the way he kept company with sinners and prostitutes. If one were to ask pastors, this would be the standard approach.

- To illustrate the second covenant-based metaphor, the chaplain explored Genesis 29, with its story about the nature of love using the relationship of Jacob, Rachel and Leah. The nature of love described here is the necessary prelude to essential themes in Exodus and in the New Testament.

Within patriarchal culture, Leah is a woman who, through no fault of her own, finds herself marginalized and unloved within the covenant of marriage. Her husband does not love her, despite his capacity for sacrificial love for her sister Rachel, but in the story God demonstrates the nature of covenantal love. In this context love is presented not as something 'done' to Leah, but as a two-way process. It actually is not merely a matter of being 'loved no matter what'. Neither is it an easy way to escape one's pain. It is necessary to articulate one's own suffering in the very specificity of one's own situation. It is specific, not general. It is exemplified in the naming of her children:

- 'God discerned my humiliation': Reuben;
- 'God has heard I was unloved': Shimon;
- 'Now my husband will love me': Levi;
- Her last son she named Judah: 'This time I will praise the Lord'.

Leah uses the names to make her stand. She states her case and moves from the role of a victim who evokes compassion to one whose experience of God evokes praise because God does not neglect, forsake, marginalize, stereotype or victimize her. She is not treated by God as a moral failure or an object for compassion. Instead, the robust covenantal relationship seen with Abraham and with Moses through their readiness to serve and to challenge God is found in Leah's story. In the Hebrew world, the early chapters of Exodus are a development of the same theme. God hears only when the people have been able to feel so much that they cry aloud.

This strong covenantal relationship is expressed powerfully in the synagogue liturgy that dates from destruction of the Second Temple. It was used in the Second Temple and so would have been familiar to Jesus and his hearers.

It begins with *Barachu*, which is similar to 'The Preface' in Christian Eucharistic liturgy: 'God *remembers* how the patriarchs acted towards him. God sustains and supports the fallen. God heals and sets captives free.'

But that isn't the end, it continues with *Kedushah*: 'Holy, Holy, Holy'. Like the prophets, the worshippers are being exposed to God 'face to face', yet standing their ground – standing in, standing for and withstanding the presence of God.

Then, finally, *Amidah*. This is to stand in the presence of God and to argue with him, plead for the marginalized, argue against the condemnation of sinners, not be afraid but stand one's ground before God and accuse priests and kings.

This is the reverse of the 'fall' of Adam. It is to be lifted up on to one's feet again, to find one's voice; not merely to be an object of pity, in need of compassion but, rather, be outward facing and notice and plead for others. It is to replicate the audacity of Moses and Abraham, the prophets and Jesus himself.

This is now the approach and calling of the chaplaincy, to restore speech, incorporate the marginal so that they may stand and argue, be empowered before God, not be silent, 'grateful' and passive.

The discussion that followed was a particularly painful and difficult one for the chaplain. He faced strong negative reactions and found no support. His personal reflection was that the members of the group focused their attention on the origin of the material being used, which meant that the issues raised around the theological metaphors he identified were not touched on and therefore avoided. This was the case even though the group included black and white, male and female, gay and straight ministers. He experienced a clear hostility towards his use of the Hebrew Scriptures and the synagogue images. In the course of the discussion, the categories 'Pharisees' and 'Jews' from a New Testament context in relation to the origin of the material were used to avoid responsibility for current failures in a way that indicated a lack of awareness of the consequences in contemporary society of such an approach to Jewish culture.

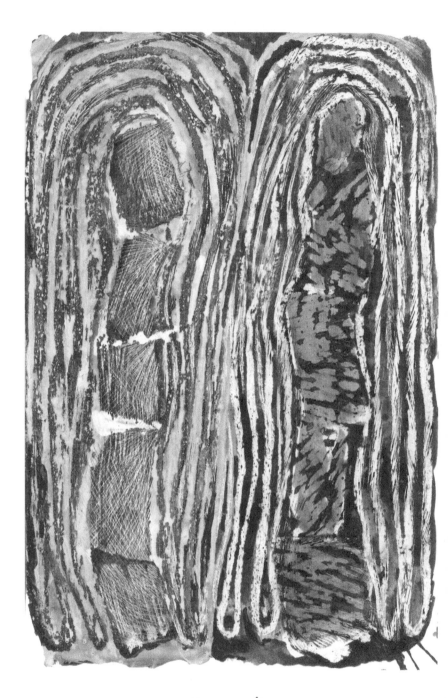

a ttune ment

Ninth testimony
In conversation with the chaplain

Our chaplain has been in post for almost a decade. His voice serves to articulate the testimony of the clients. His anguish and compassion shape the challenge he puts to the Church.

It seems to me that the pastoral approach you adopt in the chaplaincy is of supreme importance to your work.

We deal with whole people, with real lives and with burning issues. This is our starting point, and really *this* is what is of supreme importance. Any pastoral approach we have developed has been in response to encounters with our clients. We refuse to view the clients as objects of pity or as helpless 'victims'. We have learned from the clients themselves that they are determined to be listened to on their own terms. This has demanded discipline and self-emptying on our part. The best word I can find for this approach is 'attunement'.

So how is such 'attunement' achieved?

A major obstacle with any pastoral approach is to go in with a narrative and set of answers already in place. We had to drop any preconceived notions, categories and judgements (even theological ones). Our clients live extremely complex lives, and we have had to develop a way of relating to them that is open and two-way.

The foundation had to be to find a medium that would enable free exchange of information. The only way to do this was to accept the forms and definitions that the clients themselves gave to their own experiences without trying to 'solve' or undermine them. We had to drop any notion that we knew them better than they knew themselves. Clients refused to be managed, patronized or pathologized.

Next, we needed to establish a bedrock of trust. This involved allowing the clients to retain their right to control how much personal information they shared with us at any one time. Many clients do not even communicate their personal information to their employers, families, partners or friends. That they would hand us every bit of personal information to write on forms beggars belief when I look back. If we had not learned to accept information slowly as we earned their trust, there would quite simply have been *no* chaplaincy. Clients (like every one of us) are bombarded with demands for information all the time. There is no good reason why they should sign up for more of the same from us.

Surely this makes for constraints on your work as a charity – the raising of funds, the management of records, the attraction of donors, the assurance that their money is being well spent?

Our primary goal has always been to defend the clients from being 'commodified'. When clients' information or postcodes are traded for funding, the clients feel resentful or betrayed. This has certainly made my job, and that of the trustees, much more complicated. However, we try to balance protecting our clients' anonymity by acting as 'interpreters' to possible funders. It is not that we do not believe in accountability or outcomes. Far from it. It is simply that we believe in the need for these standards not to be imposed from the outside or to be experienced as intrusive. The specific situations of the clients are paramount. Any intrusion of a 'managerial' approach into pastoral work must retain that flexibility at the very least.

It sounds as if you have an approach that is simply compassionate?

Absolutely not! 'Compassion' is a seriously misused word. The 'compassionate approach' so often seems to end in what Martin Seligman calls 'learned helplessness'.[2] Clients end up being reduced to handholding and being supine in order to qualify for help. More than once when trying to discuss my work, I have unfortunately been faced with comments like, 'I do not need to hear what your clients have to say; I only need to love them.' The frustration this elicits in clients is *huge*. More importantly, it is an approach that ends without empowerment, integration or identified goals for the clients. When those engaged in pastoral care claim compassion as their private

---

[2] Christopher Peterson, Steven F. Maier, Martin P. Seligman, *Learned Helplessness: A theory for the age of personal control* (New York: Oxford University Press, 1993).

constituency, we can end up looking like emotional vampires gorging on human misery. This approach all too often looks like the strong helping out the weak (and incidentally means we have nothing to learn from our clients).

In this regard, I would like to refer again to my experience of trying to discuss my work with people engaged in pastoral work. On more than one occasion I have been met with statements that consist of 'people come to us and we decide what they need', or even that 'the purpose of pastoral work is to prove our faith is true'.

Either way, the result for the client as an object of care is the same.

So how have you handled that?

We have allowed clients to be upfront about the deep frustrations they have faced in the expression of their stories, in two ways. First, we learned to listen to *all* the ways in which clients expressed themselves. It was (metaphorically) like trying to learn many languages at once. Second, we have made it a primary goal to take all of this material and feed it back into the reflections of faith communities.

Spell that out for me.

Gladly. You will forgive me if I go on at some length about this, but it really is the heart of the matter.

Going back to the metaphor of learning several languages at once, we can glimpse the complexity of the means the clients use to express themselves.

- *Questioning* They have asked faith communities very direct questions about dicey issues such as sexuality and gender. They have done so with sincerity and openness, but certainly with a desire for answers that make sense. They have bothered to explore inconsistencies and cultural constructions surrounding these issues, or past cruelties around these matters perpetrated by faith communities. They are extremely well informed, and often very blunt. Their questioning has most often been met with aggression.
- *Emotions* Clients have expressed themselves with very strong emotions indeed. If we had in any way pathologized or protected ourselves from these we would quite simply have missed the points the clients were making. The pain and anger expressed by the clients is often towards wrongs endured. Their passion and

enthusiasm is what motivates them. Also, they express anxiety as a genuine 'existential angst' about the meaning of the situation they find themselves in. This can lead to them pointing out the inadequacies of the religious answers they are offered. If we dodge these by seeing our job as offering a 'happy ending', we again miss the point.

- *Reimagination* Clients have sought to express their experiences in symbolic representations. This has been very difficult for them, as liminal figures don't figure highly in mainstream presentations of faith. Women clients are by far the best at this. They seek out the marginal, strong women of the Hebrew and Christian scriptural heritage that presents women as unfairly judged by men, or who were stronger than 'foolish' men. Gay men experience far more difficulty in this area because the images and symbols from across the major traditions simply do not permit such reimaginings. We have had to learn to interpret and decode what clients are getting at when they resort to literature, mythology, humour, music and so on. It required a great deal of patience for us to learn to be open to the way clients were expressing fundamentally religious themes in this way. It would be easy to be dismissive or to engage in ridicule of clients when they use this material, or to be self-defensive. One example will do: when a client used a picture from the internet to laugh at an inconsistency from one faith community about 'cross-dressers', they were met with a sour-faced comment about the internet being 'a strange place', as if religious communities cannot be so at times. In any case, a small amount of patience would have got to the point the client was trying to make. Incidentally, it does us no harm to laugh at ourselves. Humour has been a major cause of clients experiencing distancing or aggression from faith communities. It seems we all take ourselves far too seriously.

- *Isolation* Most religious communities place a very high premium on membership, so those who keep their distance as a protest face harsh judgement. Most of our clients, being people of intense faith, keep a profound distance between themselves and faith communities. Partly this is because a major price of inclusion seems to consist of silence and 'not rocking the boat'. Clients have been offered inclusion at the cost of expressing the very issues that power their search for meaning in the first place. However, examination of the motives for isolation can provide communities with rich resources for reflection.

- **Rebellion** Clients' lives are messy and they are littered with loud behaviours and acts of protest around health and sexuality. Most often these elicit moralizing and judgementalism. But we have found, without in any way valorizing these actions, that at the root of them all is often a kind of 'holy foolishness'. If we but have eyes to see, then we have much to learn.
- **Instability** All our clients are people whose expressions of uncertainty change according to their communities of origin. Quite simply (as a Buddhist lama friend of mine expressed it), 'The lines on the road run right through them.' Because of this they have had to be professional 'wanderers' of a spiritual nature. This is mainly because they were initially pushed out, but also because their passionate search for meaning has led them to measure different responses and answers to the problems of life. This is simply an expression of the collapse of a metanarrative. Nowadays every city is home to many religious communities. They do not all agree and there is no safe space for any faith not to engage with the issues raised. The clients live this and present it to communities who far too often stigmatize it as 'instability'. But the grand narrative has dissolved and, with it, the sense of privilege any faith community wants to claim. The clients have a comparative knowledge of various faiths, which is frankly challenging, and they have an expressed existential anxiety that comes from knowing that *all* communities have at one time or another been implicated in marginalization and exclusion, or, again to quote my lama friend, 'They are aware all too well of the uses and abuses of religion.' Frankly, this issue only adds to the clients' uncertainty. It requires huge maturity and wisdom from faith communities to negotiate this in pastoral care for the simple reason that clients know that not all answers are the same. At its best, this can raise pastoral care above mere apologetics; all too often, however, this aspect of the clients' experience is resented.
- **'Ordinary people' syndrome** I have saved what I personally believe to be the worst till last. Any GP will tell you that a patient who has to live with a chronic condition will be among the best informed of their patients, because they will research it. However, those engaging in pastoral care seem to believe that if an experience or idea has not occurred to us, then how can the mere

'ordinary' people we care for have thought about it? Sadly, I have even encountered this among our own trustees. Our clients have had to amass a vast array of skills in order to negotiate the difficulties of their lives and faith journeys. To patronize them simply because we have not seen the need to think or change our ways is catastrophic, and is another expression of the way we distribute power unevenly in pastoral relationships.

I have used the word 'attunement' rather than 'listening' when trying to explore this matter, because this process is like trying to hear someone playing an instrument. It requires more than just therapy skills or intellectual skills, or having done a course. It requires what the clients say to resonate in our viscera. We have got to *feel* it.

It sounds as though this urgently needs to be fed into the Church's understanding of the nature of pastoral ministry.

One of the greatest expressed desires of the clients has been to see their stories fed back into the ongoing reflections of the communities who offer care to those living with HIV. Their motivation is care. They want to embed the awareness of these issues deeply as a resource for growth so that others will receive better support. It is vital for pastoral and theological training that we do not espouse grand theories that ignore exceptions to the rule. If I might steal a quote from Rabbi Lord Jonathan Sacks, 'God is in the details.'[3]

Meanwhile, our clients are viewed as anomalous. By our standards, they should *not* be sustained so deeply by their faith, yet they are. Faith communities need to understand how.

At this point it seems that pastoral care and theological principles are coming together, and in a way that is far from simple given the different faith journeys of the individual clients.

In a real sense you have put your finger on the most fundamental problem we experienced when undertaking this work. How could we express this work in principles that didn't immediately cloud the issue with rancour or sectarianism, because our clients come from many different religious faiths?

---

[3] Rabbi Lord Jonathan Sacks, 'God is in the details', *Jewish Press*, 27 Shevat 5773, 6 February, 2013.

This is the reason why we have rooted what we have fed back to religious communities solely in the clients' human experiences as a starting point for different communities to engage in dialogue with clients. We have the principle of the human being seen theologically.

However, if you were to push me on this, there are two images I would use to express our theological starting point. The first is expressed in another quote from Rabbi Jonathan Sacks: 'God does not rule slaves, *God relates to those who were slaves and who have been set free.*'[4] I use this to highlight that we can only be of service to the growth and well-being of clients when they are implicated in their own growth.

The second image would be expressed in this quote from the Orthodox Christian nun Saint Maria of Paris:

> If someone turns with his spiritual world towards the spiritual world of another person he encounters a mystery. He comes in contact with the true image of God in Man, with the very icon of God incarnate in the world, with a reflection of the mystery of God's incarnation and Divine manhood and he needs to accept this awesome revelation unconditionally.[5]

I use these quotes in no way confessionally, nor are they the only appropriate ones. However, they do express clearly the two halves of one whole. A relationship (a covenant, if you will) exists between us and our clients, a relationship which respects the pace at which the clients can grow and the issues they raise, *and* which has been experienced by us as a meeting with God.

It is the thrill that these two principles express that makes the work so amazing to engage in.

It all sounds both profound and practical, very down to earth – a reminder of the biblical Wisdom Tradition perhaps – as the basis of communication with clients.

Spot on! I used to give talks titled 'Wisdom and the problem of the love of God', but that was interpreted as intellectual. Then I tried to approach the topic using the idea of 'holiness or wholeness', again

---

[4] Believed to be from Jonathan Sacks, *The Dignity of Difference: How to avoid the clash of civilizations* (Continuum, 2002).

[5] Mother Maria Skobtsova and Jim Forest, *Mother Maria Skobtsova: Essential writings* (Orbis, 2003).

hinting at integrity, authenticity and the basic yearnings all human beings experience, but holiness seemed to be interpreted as being a colourless automaton.

Your reference to the Wisdom Tradition of the Hebrew and Christian traditions hits the nail on the head, provided it encompasses the anguish of Job or Jonah, the passion of the Song of Songs, the bravery of Queen Esther or of Daniel in the lions' den. The texts of the Wisdom Tradition deal with the anomalous examples that do not quite fit in with the grand narrative. They are the exceptions to the rules, which make us squirm slightly. Some of the texts defy a 'happy ever after' conception yet are deeply faith-filled, and they use the means of opposition, and indeed ridicule, to make their point. They all point to the passion, anguish, courage and strength that human nature can be endowed with. These texts would be (in my opinion) a perfect starting point for all chaplaincy in the contemporary world.

It is often said by academics and pastors that people only reflect on meaning when their stomachs are full, and only symbolize their spiritual lives from within the context to which they are culturally committed. Here with our clients, however, we have a group of people who sacrifice the comfort and safety of belonging because of the passion and anguish of their spiritual search. Their bravery (and rebelliousness) would find a genuine resonance in the Wisdom Tradition.

We all make mistakes and learn from them. I wonder if you would mind saying something about the mistakes you feel you have made in the work

Well, you are asking about my own perceptions so I will presume a permission to speak totally freely!

The first mistake I made was that I thought the characters of the clients I met would enrich the religious communities I had encountered in my life. To be honest, I was under the impression that many faith communities had a rather conventional, conformist and pallid membership. The clients I met were passionate, outspoken, very well informed and vibrant. I thought they would be an asset. I mentioned to a rabbi I knew that the clients' ability to keep coming back to seek faith answers despite abuse amazed me. The rabbi responded bluntly that the clients were abused because they kept returning.

I must say that caused me to lose a lot of sleep, and I realized that it is of course true: faith communities have a very definite agenda and 'client profile', and this clashes very openly with the characteristics that I had valued. No question about it.

A second mistake stems from my preference for using theological and philosophical models to seek answers to my own questions in life. I had approached the clients' stories as if they were theological or philosophical problems to be learned from and solved. That simply got in the way of hearing the hard truths the clients talked about. I learned, over time, that in order to allow the clients space to 'mythologize' their own experience, I had to train myself quite harshly to 'demythologize' my own point of view in order to relate to them properly. In the end, I discovered that the best metaphor for doing my job was one of a detective approaching evidence in search of justice, not a theologian or philosopher seeking to expound.

Disappointment and disillusionment have been experiences you must have constantly struggled with. What would you say has been the greatest disappointment?

The answer to this question is tied to my own background of having been a religious seeker. The greatest disappointment from my work (and one that will undoubtedly stay with me for the rest of my life) has been watching the facility with which faith communities repress questions that they do not wish to hear or cannot answer. The pressure brought on clients and myself to be silent when issues of abusive behaviour have been raised has been considerable. Every strategy is used to sideline and silence material that casts doubt on the self-image of faith communities. For me this will always be summed up by the attitude of a Carmelite nun from Liverpool. She was very well aware of the horrible suffering I had encountered during my work, but when there was the possibility of making a programme for television I was pressurized by her 'to be fair to the Church'. I wasn't exhorted to tell the truth or defend the clients' interests. Her concern (and the concern of many in extremely diverse faith communities) was to 'save face'. The usual excuse given is 'to protect the faith of simple believers'. Meeting that attitude so often has left a very deep scar on me.

What would you say have been the biggest problems you have faced?

The biggest has been the discouragement that comes when I have been unable to find collaborators in my work. There have been so many who simply will not follow through. Either they won't open up and discuss the complexities of life with me, or they promise things and will not deliver. The worst and frankly most depressing thing has been watching representatives of religious bodies punish the clients for my own choices. This could be by refusing funding because I personally was not able to remain a part of any church or Christian body. In one vile case, someone we approached for funding prayed over me for my 'conversion' (and still did not fund us!).

There is such a strong sense of isolation in so much that you say. Finding good collaborators is clearly a problem.

Anything I say is merely in addition to the above. It seems to me at times that people are unable to resist the temptation to 'colonize' charitable work. The external motivations so often obscure the people who are worked with. If we start any charitable work because we define the vulnerable as those who need protecting from themselves, or who are victims, then we preclude the possibility that they may need protecting from us and from our desire to demonstrate the relevance of our faith communities by 'doing good'. Someone once said to me when I posed a funding bid, 'We do this work to prove the truth of the gospel.' Honestly, what if the results we find prove, rather, the failure of communities to live up to the gospel? You can interpret my words if you wish as an attack on your faith, but it is actually an attack on your hypocrisy, and the willingness of communities that see the individuals we work with as an expedient, proving their relevance or survival by numbers.

As we close, given the strength of your own point of view, what do you do to minimize your 'stuff' influencing the clients? How do you avoid putting your views in their mouths?

That is the most pertinent of questions. There are no easy ways to avoid what you describe. The only way is to have my work constantly held up to the scrutiny of my line manager. There is constant pressure from him to reshape what I think using the criteria of intelligibility. Everything is discussed at length and any incoherence challenged from the standpoint not of faith institutions but of service to the clients. From a personal point of view, I need constantly to remind myself how my opinions have evolved and changed as a result of my contact with the clients. Therefore, my own latest theological or therapeutic craze will inevitably pass. Often, frankly, the clients have been right and I have been wrong.

The other thing has been to make sure I am responsive to the clients' needs. One example of this is their desire to utilize reading groups as a means to sharpen their self-expression. They have prevailed on me to appreciate the usefulness of fiction as a medium of naming the unnameable.

It sounds as if you are saying that you cannot do this work unless you know what you do not know, but is it really possible for you to overcome your own agenda, to jump out of your subjectivity?

I will be honest and tell you that I am only ever challenged about my own agenda by representatives of faith groups who don't like what I say. I suspect that if I were to regale them with stories of how sinful clients' lives had been turned around by embracing their particular brand of faith, they wouldn't question my methods at all. Strange that, no?

In answer to your question, however, I can only say that I am very old-fashioned. I believe it is wrong to interfere with the clients' material in any way. I resist strongly the introduction of issues clients do not mention or chopping it up to sell any faith community's line. I have kept confidential records of the conversations (which cannot be traced back to the clients) even when the material made me squirm or doubt the very existence of goodness in the world. The clients and their stories, however much they might reflect abuse, are my absolute priority. Clients' materials are neither commodities nor propaganda.

Clearly, I do not 'jump out' of the subjective belief that naming the unnameable can be an impetus to growth, as I mentioned above. Besides, let us be frank; all of life is about transcending our subjectivity. When I was at school it was called 'learning', the very concept of which brings us face to face with the idea that we might, by hard work, keep ourselves out of the space that another person or truth or even reality itself might need in order for us to relate to it as something more than an extension of our own desire to manipulate. This is about not making assumptions but allowing the client the space to tell their truth. It is when we allow the world and people to become 'other' as opposed to 'me'. This process is gradual, awkward and even painful. I find this a difficult thing to put into words, if I am honest, but ever since I was a child I have been thrilled by solving puzzles. Please believe me that I am not in any way trivializing the obstacles faced by clients (or indeed that I face myself) when I say I have approached my job as a 'whodunnit'.

It is no secret that initially I thought the clients were exaggerating. However, when I and my line manager saw the correlation between how the clients described the treatment they received for raising questions and the treatment *we* received for raising the same questions, we had evidence that the clients were not totally making it up. Added to that, the history of loading the burden of evidence on the complainant and covering up that which is openly known about institutions of all kinds (including religious ones), and we learned to infer in favour of the client. Only a complete fool would underestimate how painful this process has been to me personally as I have seen my ideas and false beliefs topple.

In the face of the extraordinary challenges we have talked about, and some we have not – for instance, the poor pay, poor collaboration, the isolation and hostility that has come with this job – what has kept you going and inspired you?

I have never experienced a perfect world. My childhood, in all aspects, resembled a cross between a play by Euripides and a novel by Dickens. Any attempt I made to understand or make sense of that world (and so process my response to it) was hampered by the frankly oppressive and overly optimistic metanarratives that dominated how my society saw itself. In trying to describe my experience with those who educated me, I was ignored or treated with embarrassment or dismissal. Experiences of cruelty or bullying were often met with silence on the part of other adults who happened to witness glimpses of it.

However, my maternal grandmother, Millicent, received my total narration with acceptance. It cannot have been easy for her to hear or accept the things I told her as true. But she made unconditional space for what I said. She treated me with understanding and kindness. I remember one incident in particular where she protected me from verbal violence by standing up to someone she loved because what they were doing was wrong. I think I became an individual that day. I was introduced to the reality of goodness and cruelty, courage and cowardice, collusion and action. I was able to reflect that just because someone was 'in authority', it didn't make their actions automatically correct. I learned that our experience can be true even when all others call it lies, and very significantly it introduced to me the idea that it was acceptable and even necessary to resist cruelty and abuse. I will tell you that a shy and sensitive boy, who until that moment thought himself useless, realized he had worth.

All of this was received by me at only about five years of age as an obligation: the obligation to do good when faced with that which was not. I know that when goodness is experienced it can change someone's world, because it changed mine for ever. Whatever I have become I owe to my grandmother; there would have been no chaplaincy in its current form without the goodness I experienced at her hands, and that is why I dedicate anything I have achieved in my work to her memory.

When I have been unable to find faith in anything else I have kept faith with that experience. Goodness is a reality even when it is a rarity. It is baffling how difficult the power of that motivation is for even clergy to grasp. Perhaps we have expected too little from people for far too long.

So much time and thought has gone into the work of this testimony and its development over the last few years. Do you have any reflection at this point about the experience?

The approach we have taken in our work has been criticized even by sympathetic people from mainline churches because it is seen as giving voice to the forces that attack religion. One minister reviewed a draft of this manuscript by saying that people who are critical of faith communities have picked up their message from false expectations instilled in them by the media, or are just voicing what society in general says. In fact, that minister went so far as to say that 'clients had too high expectations of the Church and its ministers'.

This, I believe, is to fundamentally miss the point. If I or my clients hated the Church that much, we would simply not talk to it. If we are critical of the virtue (or otherwise) that we have encountered, it is because we are looking for a life worth living, one where a community that says it represents a different vision of life from that which is available to us everywhere else in society actually does so.

I and my clients are not looking to belong to the equivalent of a football team. We are looking for a community that gives us hope for the slim existence of goodness in a world that seems to have forgotten it. In other words, all the work that this text represents is a search for the good and the true. In itself, I believe this is both praiseworthy on the part of the clients and something for faith communities to draw strength from. They simply must not presume that people will stay or join if they are not able to see that they receive the kindness and honesty that communities seek to witness to and offer the clients themselves. They must earn the clients' respect and not presume on their trust.

The final three testimonies

We have asked patience from the reader as we have progressed through what has been no easy journey. You will have noticed that all of us involved in the work (and in the preparation of this text) have continued to hit our heads against the basic problems we encountered when we first started working with clients. It has exposed you to our questions, and our imaginative and intellectual attempts to facilitate communication. It has inevitably brought you face to face with our frustrations, disillusionment and despair. It is worth repeating: this has never been an easy journey.

These next (and final) three testimonies, however, represent our move from experiment to recommendation. They are our mature insights, and we are confident in their usefulness. They are our collective suggestions for the improvement of pastoral encounters.

- **The tenth testimony** Allowing clients to narrate their experiences and insights using a medium that precludes any interference. It was literature that allowed the clients to see that the very experiences they hid most linked them to everyone else. Only when clients can face their own experiences can they process, learn from and seek meaning in them.
- **The eleventh testimony** This might be termed the 'communal' dimension. Communities that seek to minister must *be* what they say they are and must seek to understand what it is that people are seeking so determinedly.
- **The twelfth testimony** Trust can be lost as well as gained. Communities need to realize that we live in an age when we cannot just talk about 'authority' as if it is our natural right. We have no right to expect a hearing; we have to earn it. (For better or for worse, that is the way of things.)

Tenth testimony
Reading with the clients

> You think your pain and your heartbreak are unprecedented in the history of the world, but then you read. It was books that taught me that the things that tormented me most were the very things that connected me with all the people who were alive, or who had ever been alive.
>
> *James Arthur Baldwin*
> *(2 August 1924–1 December 1987)*
> *American novelist, short story writer,*
> *playwright, essayist, and social critic*[6]

Reading groups have become one of the most significant parts of the chaplain's work. He describes their development:

The reading groups started as something I tried in my own time. I had observed that the clients were simply not able to articulate their own experiences within the boundaries set by the narratives of faith communities. To put it bluntly, they faced too many prohibitions. Stories and symbols were removed from their grasp by official ownership. I got tired of highlighting this with faith communities to no avail, so I decided to find a way that did not run up against such boundaries.

The clients needed a way to make their experiences accessible to them. They also needed a way to overcome the barriers of isolation and to discover that others had suffered the kinds of trauma they had. I had kept a mental note that many of the clients were keen readers and often mentioned their latest books to me. I decided to take the risk of sharing ideas for reading with them. Luckily, the clients were hungry for a metaphorical place where their experiences could be expressed without censure. In short, both literature and reading groups allowed them to think and say things they had been told were 'forbidden'.

---

[6] Quoted in an article by Jane Howard, 'The doom and glory of knowing who you are', *Life Magazine*, 54(21), 24 May, 1963.

The end result is a series of groups that clients choose to belong to, where they discuss the things that actually bother them, where they are active rather than passive. The aim of the groups is not utilitarian or behaviourist. They simply aim to provide a space where clients can say the unnameable – and be believed. The follow-on has been striking: a noticeable re-engagement with life, management of addiction problems and, in several cases, the waking of an intellectual hunger to think and know. They are the things I am most proud of in my work.

The books that the clients have read with the chaplain are listed below. He writes:

All these books deal with complicated dystopian worlds that in their complexity and indeed stupidity actually require that we choose and think for ourselves. Very few are that 'despicable' thing that film companies call 'franchises'. All give the clients space to set their thoughts in order away from the mental colonization of the faith communities to which they belong. The interesting thing is that the gender of the protagonists does not make a difference: women and men alike respond to *all of them*.

Book list

The Mahabharata
The Rig Veda
The Way of the Bodhisattva
Richard Adams, *Shardik*
Richard Adams, *Watership Down*
Arthur C. Clarke, The *Space Odyssey* series
Arthur C. Clarke and Stephen Baxter, *The Light of Other Days*
Joseph Campbell, *The Hero with a Thousand Faces*
Philip Dick, *Do Androids Dream of Electric Sheep?*
Charles Dickens, *Barnaby Rudge*
Charles Dickens, *Oliver Twist*
Fyodor Dostoevsky, *The Brothers Karamazov*
Fyodor Dostoevsky, *The Idiot*
Neil Gaiman, *American Gods*
Neil Gaiman, *Anansi Boys*
Neil Gaiman, *Neverwhere*
Frank Herbert, The *Dune* series

Abraham Heschel, *The Prophets*
Herodotus, *The Histories*
Homer, *The Illiad* (Mitchell translation)
Homer, *The Odyssey*
Daniel Keyes, *Flowers for Algernon*
Abraham Isaac Kook, *Lights of Repentance*
Steig Larsson, *The Girl with the Dragon Tattoo* trilogy
C. S. Lewis, *Till We Have Faces*
Sinclair Lewis, *Babbitt*
Sinclair Lewis, *Elmer Gantry*
Sinclair Lewis, *It Can't Happen Here*
Sinclair Lewis, *Kingsblood Royal*
Herman Melville, *Moby Dick*
Herman Melville, *Pierre*
Herman Melville, *The Confidence Man*
Yukio Mishima, *The Sea of Fertility* tetralogy
David Mitchell, *Cloud Atlas*
David Mitchell, *The Bone Clocks*
Iris Murdoch, *The Bell*
Iris Murdoch, *The Sacred and Profane Love Machine*
Iris Murdoch, *Under the Net*
Terry Pratchett, *Masquerade*
Terry Pratchett, *Witches Abroad*
Philip Pullman, *His Dark Materials* trilogy
Rainer Maria Rilke, *Selected Poems*
Nilanjana Roy, *The Hundred Names of Darkness*
Nilanjana Roy, *Wildings*
Samantha Shannon, *Bone Season*
Samantha Shannon, *The Mime Order*
J. R. R. Tolkien, *The Hobbit*
J. R. R. Tolkien, *The Lord of the Rings*

Also especially the following:
Marina Berzins McCoy, *Wounded Heroes*
Iris Murdoch, *Metaphysics as Guide to Morals*
Iris Murdoch, *Sovereignty of the Good*
Plato, *The Symposium* (Gill translation)
Philip Pullman, *Imaginary Friends*

Eleventh testimony
Studies in diptych

This talk was given to a group of people attending the 2016 Methodist Conference at the House of Lords. The talk was written by the chaplain, but presented by the Revd Steve Penrose (Chair of Trustees).

In this talk I want to address, at their most basic, the issues that we have found to make up the HIV Chaplaincy – what we found when we reached out to clients and actually bothered to learn to listen to what they had to say. They are presented as they were offered to us – before we have been pressured to be cleverer or braver or more outspoken than we are; before we have been made to jump through hoops by funders.

The issues focus on a central question: *When does goodness stop being good?*

. . . and then the questions multiplied.

- What compromises does goodness have to make in its actions to nullify its intentions? Is it when it makes excuses for its mistakes, or covers up its collusions with power?
- Is it when goodness gets deflected into talk about 'the greater good' and ends up making excuses for crimes?
- How are we to relate to, and get beyond, claims made on behalf of goodness that clearly demonstrate minorities being used as expedient sacrifices to benefit those who claim to be undertaking good actions?
- What about when statements are made and even published that compromise so-called 'lesser' goods for politically expedient greater ones?
- Does goodness delight in, and exploit at every turn, the downfall of those with whom it finds itself in disagreement? Does it use ridicule or exaggerated imagery to caricature those who oppose it? Does goodness use the failures of those who do not fit its worldview as a means to justify itself?

- Is it ever good to judge even those you consider to be your most bitter opponent without hearing them out, without listening to the evidence they have to offer in their own defence? Does goodness roll over their voice because 'our cause is right!', or because we believe that our belief is true?
- What about goodness doing acts of good in order to 'prove' that it is good?
- How will goodness react when it finds itself implicated in hurting others, or worse? What about when it has ruined lives, or covered its mistakes up to protect its reputation? What about when it simply shouts louder than opposing voices because it is a bit stronger?
- Does goodness colonize the pain and suffering of other people in order to achieve its own aims and objectives? Does it put words into the mouths of the weak? Does it stamp off in a huff when those it does good to do not say what goodness wants to hear?
- Does goodness feel it justified to suppress raw pain or legitimate criticism in the interests of 'putting bums on pews'?
- Does goodness promise things and yet never deliver them?
- And what about the 'ethics of goodness'?
- Is it the ethic of goodness to dump a job half done in order to seek the limelight and attention that the latest 'sexy' cause offers?
- When does making inclusive or compassionate statements become unethical because it offers a false hope which is not followed through on behalf of those too weak or damaged to help themselves?
- Does goodness ever punish a group of people in need because the one who reports their need is the wrong religion, or the wrong sexuality, or is passionately outspoken?

The deadly diptych

Let us approach this more simply – from another angle.

Imagine, if you will, that, at every turn, you have been blamed for harm done to *you* by *others*.

Imagine that you have heard a thousand conflicting claims to 'ultimate' truth, all of which, amazingly, still put you at the bottom of the pile.

Imagine that your sensitivity to the basic concepts of truthfulness, goodness and kindness, of simple humaneness, finds not one hearing among those who claim that goodness is their own private constituency; that all you have to offer is misrepresented.

Now put these two stories together as panels in a diptych. There you have in a nutshell the situation we have faced in the HIV Chaplaincy.

Put these two stories face to face and what happens? They cancel each other out, because what one is desperately searching for, the other is so busily sacrificing to so-called greater, more expedient goods.

In the HIV Chaplaincy we have encountered a group of people seeking goodness at its most basic human levels. They have met with organizations so caught up in their own agendas of managing decline or of desperately shoring up their influence that they are willing to sacrifice those seekers as expedient 'eggs to be broken for the making of omelettes'.

Then you have a deadly mismatch, a diptych where hypocrisy mirrors heroism, and counterfeit mirrors the authentic.

Imprisoned in the diptych

If we at least try to agree that pastoral work at its most basic is goodness trying to *do* good, then our conceptual strategies that underlie pastoral rationale must change.

Chaplaincy among those living with HIV is not a branch of management theory. It is not a way for ailing institutions to fill their services or pews. It is not an opportunity to practise the 'do as I say but not as I do' school of theology.

The people among whom we work are not just looking to belong to a team (as one minister suggested to one of us). They are not in search of one of the many #hashtags that are available. They are not pathetic life forms who are so desperate to be loved that they do not care who offers that love.

Coming from where they do in life and having experienced what they have, what they require is simple: love that practises what it preaches; a team, if you like, that is exactly what it says on the tin! And this is long before we get on to discussing with them this or that claim to 'the truth' or descriptions of the meaning of life.

First and foremost, we have encountered in the chaplaincy those I might call 'neutral angels'. They are not interested in taking sides in wars fought in the heavens. They will test every person and ideology, every pastoral outreach programme to see if it offers glimpses of goodness through people or groups. They will do this because, frankly, they can get the other stuff for free all day every day.

Betrayed ... by 'the good'?

I was tempted to conclude by doing something we never do and quote somebody directly – not because I want to be malicious and not because they or the community they are from are the only offenders in these matters. I wanted to do it to demonstrate in an actual documented way how goodness forgets itself, compromises its objectives and is betrayed. This person is someone of profound sincerity and compassion, deeply committed to the work of the HIV Chaplaincy, with long experience of the work and a clear understanding of the unequal challenges we are up against. This person is fully aware of the suffering and injustice we have helped our clients move on from and the exhausting uphill struggle to regain health and life . . . and yet the first thought was a cover-up!

I wanted specifically to identify the person in order to drive home the point, because the words shocked me so terribly. I resisted the temptation, however, because to identify one individual, one community, one church, would give grounds for letting all the rest off the hook.

These were the words:

> I know that the Church has been party to great harm and suffering, but that is far outweighed by the good and comfort it has provided . . . When you speak publicly of HIV care, be fair . . . to the Church. Otherwise you might damage the faith of the simple people.

Admit it: this could have come out from any one of our churches – and from any one of us. How good is a community that is capable of producing that thought? What sacrifice of the innocent, what actions might such thought lead to?

Tragedy and danger come from a cover-up. It is a betrayal of goodness that produces churches with members who betray goodness. Here is an example of the horror that results. This is an extreme case, I know, but it could just as easily have come out of any one of our churches.

The client was on his way home from a church service. He was in sight of his own front door when he was aware that he was being followed. He turned around and saw friends from church, so was not alarmed and waited for them. When they met up, the so-called friends attacked our client and left him to crawl to his own front door. Somehow he managed to get into his flat.

The next day he had an appointment with our chaplain, but didn't turn up. The chaplain telephoned and thankfully the client answered his mobile. His voice was extremely weak and he sounded breathless so the chaplain went immediately around to the flat.

On seeing the client's condition, the chaplain didn't wait for an ambulance but ordered a taxi and took him straight to A&E. The client was admitted to hospital and was found to have suffered multiple injuries from the attack by his fellow church members. The client died two days later.

Where is goodness to be found in the church that owns that story?

We expect different actions from faith communities because goodness and truth beat in their hearts.

So where do we go for goodness, if 'the good' are just like anybody else?

Do you want to belong to such a community?

Do I?

Twelfth testimony
A presentation to the
Annual Methodist Conference 2017,
given by the Revd Stephen Penrose
(Chair of Trustees)

The content of this presentation was agreed in discussion with the chaplain and the Chair of Trustees.

In 2003, Methodism saw a need and responded to it by appointing me as the first chaplain to London's HIV community. In 2008, I retired and the chaplaincy went ecumenical. In 2012, we became a separate charity, although we are still heavily dependent on Methodist funding, and four of our eleven trustees are Methodists. We only have one employed chaplain, who meets regularly with 365 clients, all of whom have been traumatized by their HIV diagnosis.

When we look at the material about trauma in human beings, it comes to light that there is no really satisfactory account as to why one-third of all human beings are more susceptible to trauma than others.

To be clear, when we are dealing with any kind of trauma at all, about one-third of that one-third identifies the effects as more debilitating than others. So trauma in general is never going to be a majority report. HIV, like cancer or a leg fracture or a car accident or a marriage break-up, can be a trigger for trauma.

It is all a matter of *trust*

We in the London HIV Chaplaincy work with the one-third of the one-third of those living with HIV and who are prone to trauma: those who have suffered trauma because of their diagnosis and are unable to cope.

When we plough through the material we have gathered about dealing with those who suffer from trauma (post-traumatic stress disorder, religious trauma syndrome, complex post-traumatic stress disorder), several things come to the surface:

1 experience of one trauma will uncover one or more others;
2 those who have suffered trauma suffer anxiety when it comes to processing:
   - language;
   - the trustworthiness of their own experiences;
   - perceived acts of cruelty;
   - discrepancies between what they are told and how they are treated;
3 an experience of trauma breaches the ability to trust.

So, treatment is about establishing trust, and we approach HIV not as an exercise in marginality, not as sin or as anything else, but as a traumatic experience.

What we have laboured to do with your funding is set up a place of unequivocal *trust.*

How do we do it? How do we establish trust?

1 We respect without question the clients' own experiences. We do that by helping them to articulate, without any interference, their own experience of trauma, using one-to-one talking, by exploration with religious imagery and by group work with literature. The purpose of this is to establish confidence in the reality and truthfulness of their experience of trauma. Trauma is often linked to another in the process if the trauma moves beyond HIV.
2 In order to establish trust, we avoid the intrusion of any ulterior motives. By ulterior motives we mean any attitudes or beliefs that seek to co-modify the client or reduce them to a cheap source of 'bums on seats'. We have noticed over so many years that if clients sense any conflict of motivation between themselves and us, trust is eroded.
3 We respect the clients' personal details and data without question. Any attempt to trade on their stories or information leaves us open to suspicion of cultivating a transactional/co-modifying rather than a relational relationship.
4 Because clients have suffered trauma, we may find deeper traumas as they share their experiences and such traumas may involve mistreatment at the hands of faith communities. We never, ever make

excuses or cover up the slightest perceived failing. In other words, you will never hear us make comments such as, 'That's the media.' We never accuse clients of having false expectations of pastoral care and never expect a 'pat on the back'. To state this clearly: in an age when the mistakes and cover-ups of faith communities are manifestly plain, we re-establish trust by the only thing that works: *an apology*. We find that clients never expect infallibility but they do expect the courage to admit if and when we are wrong.

5 Those who have suffered trauma will often express that by anxiety surrounding the reliability of what they have been told. If and when matters of faith commitment arise, we employ a strictly intelligible approach, never dodging difficult questions, never bullying when we are faced with questions that we do not have an answer to, and never taking refuge in false mystery or emotional cloaking. While we respect the fact that faith cannot be fully explained, we help clients come to faith positions that respect their intelligibility and trustworthiness in both the communities and texts of their chosen creeds.

Trust involves:

- *truth*
- *truthfulness*
- *dependability*
- *genuineness*
- relationship
- humility
- respect
- vulnerability
- reality
- confidence
- self-confidence
- exploration
- questioning
- faith.

Conclusion

Clients must feel that their experiences are our absolute priority and we adapt to the way they need to be communicated with. Anybody with the slightest knowledge of either the Greek or Hebrew word for 'faith' will know that both depend on the concept of trust and truthfulness.

While we cannot account for the sensitivity to trauma, the issue of trust is a different matter. *Trust* is won or lost based on observation and experience; words and actions must fit together and complement each other, not work in opposition to each other. To re-establish trust, *our* words must match *our* actions.

The work of the chaplaincy, then, is pre-eminently one that concerns the restoration of faith.

We at the London HIV Chaplaincy commend the Methodist Church, both the Connexion and the London District, for having the courage, humility and trustworthiness to fund us as we attempt to put right a violation of trust.

Our website is <www.hivchaplaincy.com>.

Appendix: The prophetic calling?
A reflection by Kerry Tankard

'Prophecy' is a slippery term to use in church life. It has been widely claimed to give honour to too many points of view that barely transcend personal enthusiasm or resentment. Perhaps it has always been the same. Therefore, truly to test its significance and authority, a detailed and humble listening and a searching self-examination is essential. The risk of failure and the rejection of the clients' message is too great to countenance.

The Revd Kerry Tankard, a Methodist Presbyter, raises a key question to be addressed:

is the HIV Chaplaincy about sticking plasters or prophecy?

When the Church meets with those infected with or affected by HIV or AIDS, it is faced with making several decisions. It can treat people as poor victims who need sympathy and care, or as human beings who are discovering how to live positively and offering their encounters with Christ, conscious and undisclosed, to the Church as gifts of reflection on the God we worship and the Christ whom we follow.

It is clear that what the chaplain has done is to listen carefully to those he has been meeting, and what arises is both positive and disturbing. He has taken time not simply to listen and care, but also to reflect and consider what it is the Church must learn and respond to. What is God teaching the Church, and the world, in the witness of those living with or affected by HIV and AIDS?

The choice is either to patronize and consider people as clients, treating them as victims needing care, or to recognize that they are among God's chosen people and have something to teach the Church about God.

Whether or not one agrees with all his reflections is secondary to the fact that he is teasing out of the stories of both women and men destructive patterns of theology that rightly need to be challenged and critically reflected on.

As I see them, these are the questions the chaplain has been forced to consider.

- What models of God have been responsible for the infection of women and men?
- How has the Church colluded in patterns of infection?
- How has the patriarchy practised in some parts of the Church denied women a voice and caused them to be unnecessarily infected by their partners?
- How has the Church's approach to sexuality created a dehumanizing sexuality that has become rebelliously destructive?
- How must we open the Church to reformation in order to answer the Spirit of God speaking into the lives of those infected and affected by HIV and AIDS?

The safe choice for the Church is to continue to treat those living with and affected by HIV and AIDS simply as clients, commodities or victims. Social care programmes are important, but we need to be alert to the danger that at the same time they can deflect our attention from the more disturbing voice of God in the midst of this time and experience. We are not called simply to love and care, but to love and care by being the people of God.

The London HIV Chaplain has seen the need to move beyond any infantilizing model and instead to recognize the Spirit of God speaking in the stories and experiences of these women and men, and act to relay those stories, within a theological framework, to the Church so that they can be heard and responded to in our very identity, beliefs and practices.

I conclude with words from Walter Brueggemann's *Disruptive Grace*:

> Ministry in the end is not 'practical'. It is about *oracle, vision,* and *promise*, about *truth-telling* and about *hope-telling*.[7]

> Prophetic ministry consists of calling things by their right names . . . The church is a place for naming things faithfully, because euphemism is a tool for denial.[8]

---

[7] Walter Brueggemann, *Disruptive Grace* (SCM Press, 2011), p. 128.
[8] Brueggemann, *Disruptive Grace*, p. 139.

I suggest that the Church is left with the question: does it want to hear such voices and speak in language that disturbs because it is truth telling or simply to whitewash the walls as many have done before?

Kerry Tankard is a close friend of the chaplaincy and is currently the Superintendent Methodist minister of the High Peak Methodist Circuit. He trained at Wesley College, Bristol, and, prior to his move to North Derbyshire, served in the Ashton-under-Lyne and Peterborough Circuits. During his time in Peterborough he developed links with various people living with, or affected by, HIV.